# Life!

# Live It To
# WIN

## Living A Winner's Life

## Dr. Jerry A. Grillo, Jr.

FZM Publishing
Copyright 2010
Second Print 2013
By Fogzone Ministries
P.O. Box 3707 Hickory, NC. 28603

All Scriptures, unless indicated, are taken from the King James Version.

Scriptures marked NKJV are taken from the New King James Version.

Scriptures marked NIV are taken from the New International Version.

Scriptures marked Message are taken from The Message Bible.

ISBN 978-0-9891997-1-1
FZM Publishing

Printed in the United States of America.

# Table of Contents

(v)

## *INTRODUCTION*

Life is hard! It has its ups and downs, ins and outs, good times and bad. We must all survive the hardships that life produces. You must remember that seasons of crisis are merely moments in time when you compare them to all of the good things God has for you.

God's intention for our life isn't for us to suffer, nor does it include divorce, pain and debt. God desires for us to be fruitful, to multiply, to subdue and to have dominion (Genesis 1:26-28). Dominion means to rule within your domain.

Jesus made clear the awesome mandate of why He came to the earth.

*"The thief does not come except to steal, and to kill, and to destroy.* **I have come that they may have life, and that they may have it more abundantly.***"* John 10:10 NKJV

I once heard someone say that Jesus didn't come to the earth to get people to Heaven. Now when I first heard this I did what most of us do who have been raised in church. I became a little uncomfortable. My mind wanted to argue before I had even given the person time to explain. After hearing him out, I found that his statement was scriptural, especially according to John 10:10. Jesus didn't come to get us to Heaven, but to give Heaven back to us so that we could become a powerful tool for the interests of God on the earth. Let me show you a verse that gives more meaning to what I am saying.

*"But you are those who have continued with Me in My trials. And I bestow upon you a kingdom, just as*

*My Father <u>bestowed</u> one upon Me, that you may eat and drink at My table in My kingdom, and sit on thrones judging the twelve tribes of Israel."* Luke 22:28-30 NKJV

Do you see the word "bestowed"? That word means channel. Jesus said He was going to channel the Kingdom through us. This is a very powerful thought. We are not just saved to make Heaven. We are mediums, channels for the Kingdom of Heaven to flood the earth. The old saying makes sense to me, *"If God can get it through you, He will get it to you."*

Heaven was off limits to earth and earth was off limits to Heaven. These two places had no connection. Jesus came as a bridge that gave us access once again. We must discover what is keeping us from becoming that bridge, that channel.

Most humans have the same basic fears:
1. Fear of criticism
2. Fear of rejection
3. Fear of failure
4. Fear of pain
5. Fear of being wrong
6. Fear of change
7. Fear of the unknown

Everyone is afraid of something; from the grown man afraid to show emotions because he was persuaded that real men don't cry, to the woman who won't open up because she's afraid to be humiliated. We all have fears to face and we must be willing to identify and face these fears if we are going to defeat them. We can't overtake them or destroy them until we are at least honest with ourselves about having them. We must find their origin.

## HEAVEN DOESN'T OPERATE ON FEAR

No enduring power can have its origin from fear. Any power that is built on fear is bound to crumble and disintegrate. You will never win or overcome your crisis using the motivation of fear. This has been the biggest mistake in the church. We have used the power of fear to motivate people to change. The Kingdom of Heaven doesn't operate on fear, but love and faith. The greatest of these is love and love cast out all fears.

*"And now these three remain: faith, hope and love. But the greatest of these is love."* I Corinthians 13:13

*"There is no fear in love. But perfect love drives out fear, because fear has to do with punishment. The one who fears is not made perfect in love."* I John 4:18

God didn't send his son to condemn us but to bridge the heavenly powers back to, and in, the earth. For God so loved the world - not the cosmos, not the laws of physics, not the mountains and the streams – but us! God loves the people He created and has given us the power to rule, to have dominion, to subdue and to multiply. We were made in His image and in His likeness. We only have one life to live and God expects us to live it to WIN!

When I sat down to pen this book I was going through some major fears and crisis myself. I have experienced a lot of stress in my life; not because there is this great big devil opposing me but because I simply made bad decisions about whom and what I allowed to be connected to my life.

Stress may be the proof you're moving where

God isn't leading. On a flight to Brooklyn, New York, I started thinking about the stress that relationships can cause; thus the reason for this manuscript. I took out my yellow pad and began to pen keys on how to have a stress free life, a stress free ministry and a stress free business. I believe these keys are the formula to a winner's world.

I've come to the realization that most of my pain was self-inflicted. I should have qualified my actions better... my relationships better... my spending better. I should have asked more questions. I should have listened to those around me. I should have been better at recognizing the end of one season and the beginning of another.

This book is going to help you tremendously as I reveal the mindset behind my own mistakes. I want to help you not to make these same mistakes in your life. Isn't that what we are supposed to do; help others become better people through our experiences? Pain is a teacher within itself, and we should share with others how not to make the same painful decisions that we have.

This is what true purpose is: being willing to expose the areas where you have failed to help others accelerate their success. The Kingdom of God would advance much faster if we all would take on this way of living. Each one would reach one.

Prepare to conquer your fears! Prepare to walk in abundance! Prepare to experience a life of favor! Get ready to live the life of a WINNER!

When you travel to a different country you must have a passport. A passport gives you accelerated access to another place because it declares you have been identified by another nation. You are a citizen of another government. I want the information written within this book to wake up your understanding that you have been identified by the Kingdom of God. You have been given access to all of Heaven and have diplomatic immunity. You do not have to accept what the world says about your life. Read slowly... Read continuously... Teach these life principles to those around you. The next chapters will help you seize the moments and reclaim your identity. I promise they will change your life and the lives of those around you.

Remember, *you only have one life to live. LIVE IT TO WIN!*

Dr. G

## CHAPTER ONE

# KNOW AND GROW YOUR DIFFERENCE

*D*ifference means you are not like anything around you. You are not the same; you are distinct from others.

I can tell you by experience that this could be the most important key to a stress free lifestyle. I have spent a lot of wasted energy and time trying to be someone else; watching the life of others and wishing I was them. This is not to say that we can't watch and learn from others. The problem exists when we sacrifice who we "are" to become someone we are not.

Paul said in Romans 12:2 that we are to not be conformed to this world but transformed by the renewing of our minds (paraphrased). A conformed person is a person who has a copy mindset. They are always conforming to and being controlled by what is around them. A copy mindset lives the life of conformity.

A transformed life is a person who has a creative mind set. This person is no longer trying to compete with and copy what others are doing. They want to create; create success, create achievements, create joy where there is sadness, and create peace when the storm is at its worst. A transformed or creative mind is a mind that has discovered its difference.

How do we transform? By renewing our minds daily and washing our minds with creative thoughts of goodness and mercy. We renew our minds by allowing the creator (God) to have access to our entire mind and ideas.

## KNOWING YOUR IDENTITY CREATES A TRANSFORMED MIND SET

Think for a moment. Do you really know who you are? Do you understand your purpose? Why are you here? What are you here to do?

> **LIFE PRINCIPLE**
> *You Will Never Rise Above Your Own Self Portrait. You Will Never Be More Than The Person You Think You Are.*

People who want to be someone else have a poor self portrait of themselves. Your self-portrait is very important to a stress free life.

### LIFE IS A PROCESS

Most people have to grow into and learn their difference. Very few people change overnight. It takes a while for most of us to discern and grow our difference. We are all products of the imprintings of our past. Events and important people, or those we thought were important, from our past shape our understanding of who we are and what we are becoming. Wrong people in our lives can cause our self-portrait to become distorted instead of building and shaping our identity to be who we were created to be. This is the reason so many copy others instead of becoming who they are meant to be.

The proof that a person hasn't yet discerned their difference is that they are always wounded and offended. Someone who is always mad or hurt could have little or no self-confidence. They lack the understanding of their purpose and reason for being alive. They try to be someone else. You are never a good copy. You will always be a great original.

Discovering you have a self-portrait problem doesn't make you a bad person; it starts your healing. Don't allow an atmosphere of condemnation to enter your life and permit feelings of guilt and shame to be on the menu of the day. Shame is how the enemy keeps us from exposing our weaknesses and flaws. Shame keeps us in bondage to our past.

I want to give you a scriptural pill:

*"Instead of your shame you shall have double honor, and instead of confusion they shall rejoice in their portion. Therefore in their land they shall possess double; everlasting joy shall be theirs."* Isaiah 61:7 NKJV

There is a song that we sing that goes something like this: *"I'm trading my sorrows, I'm trading my shame. I'm laying them down for the joy of the Lord...."*

How about you? Are you going to make a trade? Why not do what you need to do? Let go of that shame and allow truth to correct you so that you can get on with your life and discern your difference.

## LIFE PRINCIPLE
*Something You Need Is Usually Hidden In Something You Don't Like Or Can't Stand.*

I was standing in my closet, staring at my suits, preparing to get dressed to head out to a meeting. After trying on two suits to find the one that fit, I was mad and upset with myself for allowing my weight to get out of control.

I had gained some weight and was now what I call the "2 to 1" method to getting dressed; try on two to find the one that fits. I was so upset that I started complaining to the Lord about my problem, hoping to gain some spiritual reason as to why I had gained weight. As usual my wife spoke up and said, *"If you stop eating late, choose better foods and of course exercise more, you wouldn't have to worry about gaining so much weight."* I didn't want to hear it. I already knew the answer to my question. Hidden in what I hated was the thing I needed the most; exercise and better eating habits.

If you are a person who doesn't know your difference, you probably won't be able to change properly and become healthier. Most of what you need to grow and change is hidden in someone you probably can't stand - those who enter your life who are willing to correct you. A mentor is usually someone who at first will frustrate you... stretch you... pull you... correct you; all these moments create seasons of pain. You are going to have to weather a season of discomfort to extract what is necessary to change and grow. Are you willing to be taught truth by someone you don't like? Can you discern that the information you need may come from someone you can't stand, and if so, can you stay around to grow?

The difference between non achievers and achievers is the ability to do what is uncomfortable to build their self-worth and grow their difference. The proof of a secure identity is to discern and embrace your difference.

Difference is what makes you important. If you don't know your difference you can't grow your difference. Many sit in our churches stagnate. They have stopped changing and growing. These people are anointed and have callings on their lives to do great things for God. They possess the ability to help others who need change if they would only discover their difference!

> ## LIFE PRINCIPLE
> *The Proof Of A Secure And Healthy Identity Is To Discern And Embrace Your Difference.*

Their inability, or unwillingness, to see their difference hinders them from fulfilling their destiny. Matthew 2:14 says, *"Many are called, but few are chosen."* The chosen are those who show up. The chosen are those who know their difference and are willing to grow that difference so they can advance the Kingdom of God to its fullest potential. The called are many; but it is the few that choose to change.

God is a God of change, yet He is always the same. The Word of God declares that He is a God that changes not. However, He can be new every day to us. The proof that God is present is that change takes place. You may come in His presence messed up... you may come in with wounds...you may enter sick...but the proof that God was there is that you didn't stay messed up, sick and wounded.

Genesis chapter thirty-two tells us a story about Jacob and an experience he had in the presence of God:

> *"And when he saw that he prevailed not against him, he touched the hollow of his thigh; and the hollow of Jacob's thigh was out of joint, as he wrestled with him."* Genesis 32:25

Something woke up within Jacob as he wrestled with God; his difference was revealed. The prince in him woke up. The prince was always within him but as long as he could not get past what he was called *(Jacob meant "Trickster")* and what others thought and spoke about him, Jacob would always remain in the prison of a "copy mind set". When the truth was revealed and his difference materialized, the prince that had always been in him awakened and changed Jacob's life.

Jacob was about to meet Esau, a person in his past that he had deceived and lied about. Jacob was about to have an encounter with his past. God knew without a healed mind of knowing his difference, Jacob would have met his past with the same attitude that he always had. He would have wanted to compete. He would have wanted to prove something to Esau, but when Jacob awakened his difference, he no longer felt the need to prove himself to anyone, not even his past.

The same is true for you and me. We will be healed of what use to hold us back when we discern and embrace our uniqueness.

Years ago I attended a conference in Orlando, Florida. My ministry wasn't where I wanted it to be and I was becoming increasingly depressed and disappointed. This conference was helping me, but before it was over I got hit with a hard blow. I was standing out in the foyer when I noticed this awesome car drive up. This car said success. Then all of a sudden the person that stepped out of that car was someone I knew. Like most, I thought he must be using someone else's car. After all there was no way this guy who is ten years younger than me could afford this kind of vehicle. I was wrong.

I did what you're supposed to do. I greeted my friend and hugged his neck, but deep down inside the anger, the hurt and the disappointment were raging. I placed on my face a nice, fake smile but all the while I was crying within. Here's the crazy thing. All these hurts and feelings weren't his fault. He was doing what all of us are trying to do...succeed.

When your identity is failing you, all you can do is focus on the success of those around you. This stops the creative process in you. This causes you to live life in comparison mode and not creative mode. God didn't create us to live life having to compare ourselves with others. God created us to be who we are and that's all we can really be.

My friend began to let me know how wonderful his life had become. His ministry was booming. He was preaching all over the country. He was hanging out with all the "big" preachers.

I left his presence, went straight to my room, fell on the bed and cried out to the Lord: *"What's wrong with me?"* I shouted! *"Why? Why haven't I received my harvest? I sow...I give... Lord, I'm trying to do all that you tell me. What's going on?"*

While I was lying on that bed and crying to the Lord, He impressed on me this: *"Son, I can't bless you like I want to bless you until you wake up the real you. The proof you don't know who you are and what you are here to do is jealousy. When you know your difference you will grow that difference and you will be blessed."*

## LIFE PRINCIPLE
*You Are Never A Good Copy, But You Are Always A Wonderful Original.*

The Lord started my healing process that day. Let me express to you that life is much better when you find your difference. Life becomes so joyful when you understand that you don't have to be what everyone else is and do what everyone else is doing to feel secure and happy.

Life is too short to spend most of it discerning your worth by what you are feeling...seeing...hearing or experiencing. God made us and we are fearfully and wonderfully made. Even the Psalmist wanted to know what man was:

*"What is man that you are mindful of him, the son of man that you care for him? You made him a little lower than the heavenly beings and crowned him with glory and honor."* Psalms 8:4-5 NIV

I love this verse because it states clearly how much value God places in us. Man is so valuable to God that his mind is full of us. We are always on his mind and in His heart. Even the angels in Heaven notice that God keeps His attention on us. I'm sure that the angels can't grasp why God is so in love with us; seeing that we are so fragile and flawed and yet God keeps His mind full of us.

God has crowned us – flawed and fragile beings- with His presence, His glory and His power. WOW! Do you see your value now? Do you understand why you need to discern and embrace your difference? You and I are here to be, and do, something for the King (Jesus). It doesn't matter if your difference is preaching to millions or cleaning your church each week. You are successful in the eyes of God when you discover and embrace your difference!

## THE LAW OF CENTER

This is a powerful law for discerning the value of difference. Where does self-awareness live? It lives in the center of your will, your mind and your psyche. *What's happening in you is deciding what's happening around you.* Man is so conditioned to believe only what he sees around him. However, the power of what's around you is affected by what's happening in you. I've said it before; your mind is your world.

## LIFE PRINCIPLE
*Never Define Who You Are By What You Are Feeling, Seeing, Hearing Or Experiencing.*

Look at the earth. The external things sit on the surface of the earth because of the law of gravity. Without gravity everything would be floating around and off of the earth's surface, including you. Where does gravity come from? It comes from the center of the earth. So what you see on the surface of the earth is really produced by its center. If the earth's center stops operating, its external world will become disruptive and out of order. The same is true for you and me. If we want to control our external world, we need to focus on our internal center. What's happening in me is deciding what's happening around me. That center is my difference.

Some have called it the law of attraction. I like to call it the law of center. Don't let some dead, religious, unlearned person talk you out of understanding the attitude of your center. What you are saying, thinking and feeling is causing those things to stay attached to you.

**GOD HAS DEPOSITED GREATNESS IN ALL OF US.**

The truth is that God has placed the power to do great things in all of us. He has made us in His image and in His likeness. This is the law. When God hides His greatness within something, He will not rest until He has brought those things to pass which He has hidden. Get ready! You are about to be snatched to center stage. God is about to reveal those things that will promote you. The first thing that is going to promote you is your difference. Stop being ashamed of who you are and walk free from the bondage of trying to please everyone around you. If you don't know your difference, you will live a life full of stress. Life will become a fish bowl of pain, disappointment and grief. If you want to avoid this fish bowl, do so by praying that God, through the Holy Spirit, will reveal to you your difference; the reason you are here!

**FACTS ABOUT DIFFERENCE:**

- **Difference is what makes you important.**
- **Difference is where your identity flourishes.**
- **Knowing your difference will cause jealousy, anger and bitterness to cease.**
- **Celebrate, market and sell your difference.**
- **Your difference is a money magnet.**

# CHAPTER TWO

# DISCERN WHO BELONGS IN YOUR LIFE

$\mathcal{R}$elationships can be very costly, especially wrong ones. The inability to qualify those you let in and around your life can cost you in many areas including your peace... your passion... your focus... your money... your health.

Wrong people can be friends you have made, a family member you can't control, a boyfriend or girlfriend that is pressuring you to do and be what you don't want to. Wrong people can be those you are mentoring who choose not to respect the boundaries of the relationship.

## LIFE PRINCIPLE
*When People Show You Who They Really Are...Believe Them. They Are Not Lying.*

I can testify that many of my problems in life were birthed because I allowed the wrong people to stay around too long. After much pain, I came to realize that this was one of my greatest weaknesses; I allowed the wrong people to stay connected to me to gain wisdom and glean from my experiences. These people weren't with me but serving their own agendas. They caused nothing but havoc and pain in my life and church and proved their disloyalty, when they left my ministry, with anger, lies and deceit.

Do you desire a stress free life? Start right now by qualifying everyone who is in your life. It may not be what's going on in your life that's hindering your blessing but whom you have allowed to stay in your life that is stopping the flow of favor and promotion.

God withheld the rest of the promise until Abraham let Lot go. I have often wondered how much blessing and promotion I have cost myself by not discerning who was in my life to use me or to learn from me.

*"They went out from us, but they did not really belong to us. For if they had belonged to us, they would have remained with us; but their going showed that none of them belonged to us...."* I John 2:19

I love this verse. Those who belong to us will be there in the end. Stop trying to keep everyone around by pleasing them. Be yourself and if those around you don't like who you really are then they don't belong to you. Let them go. Make room for those who God is trying to place in your life who will be with you. They will support and care for you, and they will not take your love, teaching, time and effort for granted.

Learn quickly that not everyone belongs in your life. Wrong relationships are so dangerous. I've seen it over and over again. Someone will start changing and getting their life worked out. Then I will see them with a new friend, boyfriend or girlfriend. They start falling down to the level of those new relationships they have made within weeks.

## LIFE PRINICPLE
### *Allow Wrong People To Leave!*

You must recognize that there is a difference between friendships and those God is connecting you to for your future. It's possible to have friendships that are not connected to those who are not connected to your future. **Friends are just friends** and they are usually not in your life to help you succeed to your next season. You rarely mentor or teach your friends what you've learned because most people don't want to learn from their friends.

What I am about to say may make you uncomfortable but that's not my intention. It's not necessarily a fact of life, but I believe it's true for most of us if we can admit it.

I can live without friends. I can't get into my future without connections. Connections create advancement and growth. I connect with those around me who are reaching for the same goals. A protégé connects to me in an effort to reach my season. I connect to a mentor so that I can reach for their season. These connections are more vital than friendships!

There are those who are with me, those who are ahead of me and those who are following me. This sequence is how we work the law of two. One person is only strong enough to conquer a thousand, but our strength increases with connection and we can conquer ten thousand (Deuteronomy 32:30). The Bible says a threefold cord is not easily broken.

*"Though one may be overpowered, two can defend themselves. A cord of three strands is not quickly broken."* Ecclesiastes 4:12 NIV

People come and go. You have to make room in your heart to allow people to leave. If you don't you will become angry, bitter, hurt and, in some cases, so wounded that God will stop using you. ALLOW WRONG PEOPLE TO LEAVE!

Right people in one season can become the wrong people in the next season. We have to understand that people will always be coming and going in our lives. We must understand this or we will be so focused on those exiting our lives that we miss the right person who is trying to enter. I have done this a lot in my life. My insecurities caused me to keep reaching when I needed to let go. You must allow the Holy Spirit to heal insecurities such as rejection, betrayal and abandonment or you will hold on to wrong relationships and the right ones will never come.

---

## LIFE PRINCIPLE
*The Most Dangerous Person In Your Life Is The Person Who Feeds Your Doubts.*

---

Let me allow you to enter my world. I am not writing this because I've mastered this principle. At this very season in my life I am dealing with the law of release after allowing someone to stay too long. This person isn't evil or bad. I am more at fault than they are. I should have read the signs. I should have opened my eyes. I should have noticed that things in them were different. Remember my life principle. *"When people show you who they really are, believe them."*

Wounded people have a hard time confronting others. When we fail to confront, we fail to make proper decisions. When we fail to make decisions, we make the decision to fail.

I didn't react fast enough in this situation which would have allowed them to be sent to another place without so much stress.

*Hesitation is a killer to comfort.* People are not evil, unsaved or wrong just because it's time for them to leave; however, they might do wrong things if they stay too long. This could be our fault for not discerning they needed to leave earlier. You will eventually fail if you don't remove wrong people.

Remove them swiftly and as easily as possible. No matter what, when their time is up, it's up! There is nothing you can pray or do to keep them there if God wants them to leave. Just allow the door to open without anger, worry or bitterness. Allow the Holy Spirit to help them leave and it will be peaceful.

If you are discerning that a season of connection is up, react quickly; prepare a bridge so that there will be smooth transition in both lives. I believe that God has already prepared your next connection. Your Boaz is already on the way.

Eve's future changed forever the moment she gave her ear to the serpent. As soon as Adam turned his head and gave his ear to Eve, his future changed forever. When we allow wrong people to speak to us then we are giving them a legal right to control us. Let me add this; right people speaking wrong things can also damage your future. Discern truth immediately.

## LIFE PRINCIPLE
*Discern Those Close To You That The Enemy Is Influencing.*

I heard someone once say that the difference in people is who they've decided to believe. Silence the wrong people. Silence them quickly. Silence them before they persuade you to do something that is going to cost you dearly. What if Adam and Eve would have silenced the wrong voice?

FACTS ABOUT RELATIONSHIPS:
- **Wrong relationships will drain your energy.**
- **Wrong relationships will break your focus.**

- **Wrong relationships can destroy your values and character.**
- **Wrong relationships can create seasons of anger and bitterness.**
- **Wrong relationships anchor you to your present. Right relationships open doors for your future.**
- **Wrong relationships can rob you of your promises.**
- **Wrong relationships can hinder the season for right connections to happen.**

Discern quickly who the enemy is using to stop your growth. When you hang out with them you are letting others know that you are in approval of their lifestyle. The word of God says that bad company corrupts good morals. *(I Corinthians 15:33)*

**THE LAW OF ASSOCIATION**

I can tell who you are and what your future will be by observing who you hang out with. Your friends tell me all I need to know about what you think about yourself. I heard a story one time about the law of association.

**LIFE PRINICPLE**
*I Can Tell Who You Are By Who You Hang Out With.*

*A young lawyer graduated school and moved to a small town, started a practice, hired a secretary and sat in his office waiting for clients. After a few days and no clients, not even one phone call, he became frustrated and discouraged.*

*One day the phone rang. It was the old lawyer that had been in that town all his life. He had built a healthy business and was one of the most respected attorneys in town. He asked the young attorney, "How's business going?" The young attorney replied, "Not so good." The older attorney said, "I want to help you son. I want to help you get your practice off and running. Let's go to lunch tomorrow. I will pick you up, and we will go together."*

*Around 12 o'clock the next day the old attorney showed up just as he promised. "Are you ready?" In which the reply was, "Oh yeah."*

*They walked out the office complex and the old attorney said, "Let's walk to the old diner."*

*"Why?" replied the young attorney.*

*"Trust me," said the other attorney. So they ate their meal and walked slowly back to the young attorney's office hours later. The old attorney shook his hand and said, "There son, that's all you need. Have a great business."*

*"But you haven't given me one word of mentorship... you haven't shared with me one client... How is this going to help me get phone calls and clients?"*

*The old attorney replied, "Just sit back and see." The next day, the phone rang off the hook and the young attorney's business took off. He became the second largest law firm in that town.*

This is the power of the Law of Association. The old attorney had established himself as a good, fair and successful lawyer. When the people saw the young lawyer walking with him down the street and eating lunch with him, they automatically assumed that he would be just like the old lawyer. Right relationships are the only relationships we need to be looking for. We are not going to discover the right people if we keep allowing the wrong ones to stay around us.

I wish I would have known this earlier in my life. I wish someone would have mentored me in this one law. It would have saved me so much pain and stress. It's a terrible place to be in a wrong relationship. It's a worse place to be in one and not know how to get out.

Have you ever noticed that when you're trying to live right and do right that certain people can create a season of confusion? One person can enter your atmosphere and truth goes out the window and all you have around you is confusion. A deceiver is present. Trust me! You can tell a deceiver is in the room by monitoring how much confusion is in that room.

I have dealt with many deceivers in my life and ministry. I could tell you several occasions where a staff member or leader would add their comments while I was in the process of mentoring and teaching those around me. They didn't sound like they were attacking me, but confusion entered the room when they finished speaking.

## LIFE PRINCIPLE
*Confusion Could Be The Proof That A Deceiver Is Present.*

Those who have done this eventually left my life causing pain and sorrow. I should have recognized that a deceiver was in the midst the moment confusion entered.

The Bible says that every evil work is present when there is confusion *(James 3:16)*. Confusion is deadly. The word confusion means puzzlement or to be in a state of disorder. Confusion births disorder. Confusion creates an atmosphere where people can no longer distinguish between what is right and what is wrong.

**KEYS THAT STOP CONFUSION:**

1. *Clear and precise truth will expose and eliminate confusion.*
2. *Silence the person who is distorting the flow of knowledge around you.*
3. *Discern those who carry confusion with them. Remove them swiftly.*

This is the most valuable principle you can learn. You are not responsible to change a deceiver... only to discern them. When you discern a deceiver, move quickly away from them. Move swiftly before you are caught up in their deception.

**LIFE PRINCIPLE**
*I'm Not Required To Change A Deceiver Only To Discern Them.*

Deceivers will only stay loyal as long as they are gaining what they want. They will immediately turn on you as soon as you have to make a decision that creates a season of drought. Fire a deceiver quickly. I don't care if it's a family member; move swiftly away from deceivers.

**How do you know a deceiver?** Someone who thinks their agenda is more important than yours. I have waited too long so many times to address and confront those around me with hidden agendas. It has cost me dearly! This is not being mean. Trust me, you will build a stress free life when you discern and move quickly away from deceivers.

I have wasted so much time and energy by trying to fix those who were unfixable. Some people will never change no matter how much you try to help them. You have to turn them over to God. It's not that they can't change; they just won't. They will not let you in long enough to correct and fix their brokenness. I know that this sounds hard, but if you want to live stress free, let go and let God have them. Don't even keep hanging around with these people; just let them go.

I have spent sleepless nights trying to fix unfixable people. I had a person in my life for many years, yet I saw no change in him. I had to break connection. When helping you is hurting me; it's time to stop helping you.

## LIFE PRINCIPLE
*Some People Are Unwilling To Be Fixed.*
*Stop Counseling Those Who Will Not*

*"And whoever will not receive you nor hear your words, when you depart from that house or city, **shake off the dust from your feet.** Assuredly, I say to you, it will be more tolerable for the land of Sodom and Gomorrah in the day of judgment than for that city!"* Matthew 10:14-15 NKJV

I have given countless hours trying to help people who didn't really want it. You will be drained and become angry, frustrated and stressed when you spend too much time giving information to someone who doesn't want to learn. Stop trying to mentor those who are supposed to leave.

# CHAPTER THREE

# QUALIFY BEFORE YOU PROMOTE

*W*hether you're running a business, pastoring a church or just trying to live life, qualify everyone. Qualify before you promote a person to a leadership position. Qualify before you decide to take your relationship to the next level. Qualify before you get married. Qualified people make the grade and they are fit for the next level. They meet the criteria.

---

**LIFE PRINCIPLE**
*Not Everyone Who Wants The Position Is Qualified For It.*

---

You need to be more conscience of those you promote if you want to have a stress free life. I can trace so many of my failures and pain in the ministry to hiring eager people. **Eager doesn't mean ready**. Eager doesn't mean qualified. It's not that you can't have qualified people who are eager but don't overlook skill just because you see passion. Passion and eagerness may get you noticed, but it will be experience and skill that keep you noticed. People rarely become successful just on eagerness. However, skill alone can promote you. Eagerness helps you get noticed and promoted sooner.

Churches will hire and promote people without background checks; however, the world doesn't operate in this manner. Most corporations require an application or resume to even be considered for a job. Not so in the church. We promote eagerness! We find someone who is enthusiastic, passionate and impatient and place them in a position of influence only to find out they were not ready. We don't spend the right time qualifying them for their position. Disqualify those who become angry when you are trying to qualify. Their wound and offense is a reaction and a clue that they are not ready.

Don't make appearances more important than content. Many have the entry of the palace, but when they reveal their content, they are nothing more than a hut.

Have you ever noticed someone right off the bat that seems to have it going on? They come in excited, always quoting the Bible and always happy. Nothing ever seems to get them down. Well, let me tell you the truth. No one is that happy! They are concealing their true self. Trust me on this. They are hiding who they really are.

I once saw a book in a bookstore entitled, *"Everyone's Normal Until You Get to Know Them"*. That is the truth.

If we don't qualify, in the beginning of a relationship, we may think we are marrying, hiring or hanging out with someone who has been trained in the palace. You need to get to know someone first or you might find yourself waking up in a nightmare, connected to the mind set and attitude of a "HUT" instead of a "PALACE".

Qualify everybody. This gives you the information that you need to know to place people in and around your life.

## LIFE PRINCIPLE
### *Entry Of The Palace... Content Of A Hut!*

Those who don't discern your value disqualify for your relationship. If the person you've allowed around you can't see your value then they will never promote you in your absence.

Don't forget this. People act different in your presence than they do in your absence. If someone in your life doesn't esteem you in their presence then they sure are not going to in your absence.

The world is a stage and everyone is trying to find someone to dance for. We want to shine for the people who value, appreciate and honor all that we do. Many are entering your life to use you instead of honor you. Preachers and ministers, please understand that there will be more people that want to use you than want to honor you.

## LIFE PRINCIPLE
*Discern Who Values You And Who Is Using You.*

I can only imagine how Jesus must have felt after preaching all day, giving up food, water and personal needs, to make sure the people were spiritually fed. He must have cried in silent frustration, after all He said and did for them, when He realized that most of them didn't want Him. Most of them wanted what He could do for them. They were exploiting His gift and not taking it and growing to their full potential. They did not value Him; they were using Him. When you read the Bible, you will discover that Jesus eventually left the crowds and used His time for training the few. Jesus knew the few that honored Him was enough to carry on what He had started.

Learn this one thing and you can erase years of frustration: ask a lot of questions, especially when you are trying to decide how to position a person around you. Questions reveal what is trying to be hidden.

- *Questions are the only answers that bosses will respond to.*
- *Questions are the bridges to greater knowledge.*
- *Questions cure ignorance.*
- *Questions become highways that knowledge and information travel on.*

Don't be afraid to ask questions. Watch the response of people as they answer you. People who become agitated by questions are hiding something. Think about the times you wished you would have asked more questions. Maybe you would not have had to suffer as much through certain relationships if you would have just asked more questions.

Many Christians have yet to experience their blessings because they simply haven't asked for them...

*"You do not have, because you do not ask God. When you ask, you do not receive, because you ask with wrong motives, that you may spend what you get on your pleasures."* James 4:2-3 NIV

Don't underestimate the power of questions! You must master asking the right questions for your growth to wisdom.

## LIFE PRINCIPLE
*Questions Reveal A Person's Hidden Agenda.*

My mentor has taught me many great things about how to act and react around great people. The one thing he has always been a stickler about is asking questions. Ask questions instead of talking about your accomplishments when you're in the presence of someone who can promote you. Ask about their life. Ask about how they accomplished their success. Make your questions about them and you will be added to their list of people that they want to help.

The whole purpose for qualifying is to make sure that what you are deciding to add, to your life, ministry or business, is going to be good for you and not destroy you.

The importance of qualifying reminds me of the story of Jonah and the whale. Jonah decided to disobey God and flee one place to another. Hoping to escape God and His instruction, Jonah boarded a ship. God saw Jonah running from the instruction and sent a storm to stop him. The people on the boat started throwing their possessions overboard as the wind and the waves tossed the ship around. They knew nothing about Jonah's act of disobedience. They were attempting to please God by sacrificing what they had, until Jonah informed them that it wasn't what was on their ship but who was on their

---

**LIFE PRINCIPLE**
*It's Not What You Don't Have, But What You Have Added To Your Life That Could Be Killing You.*

---

ship.

You can head into the path of a storm that isn't scheduled for you when you don't qualify those around you.

Water, H2O, is two parts hydrogen and one part oxygen. When you add one more part of hydrogen to the mix you no longer have water, but hydrogen peroxide. Hydrogen Peroxide is poisonous!

One wrong addition to the equation is all that it takes to kill you.

Please qualify....qualify... qualify everyone, every decision and every relationship. Your whole life could depend on it.

I once asked a friend who had worked on Wall Street, *"What was the greatest thing you learned while working there?"* His response was revealing. *"Evaluate every investment for its return. If your investments are not bringing you a return, then change them."*

## LIFE PRINCIPLE
*Continually Evaluate The Returns You Receive From Every Investment You Make In Others.*

We should evaluate what return we are gaining from every investment we make into people. You can save yourself a whole lot of stress by following this one major principle; make every relationship produce. Make every person you pour into, become accountable at some point, to return into you what you have been so faithfully pouring into them. You will come up bankrupt in that relationship if you don't. Relationships are a give-and- take process. You will reach into your pockets and come out emptyhanded if you are always doing the giving.

Your ability to ask the right questions and qualify those around you will protect you from frustration and stress.

# CHAPTER FOUR

# CONQUER YOUR ENEMY

*M*y dear friend, Dr. Todd Coontz, invited me to be a guest on his television program and talk about my book, *"Saved but Damaged: Keys to Emotional Healing."* One of the questions Todd asked me was what I thought was the number one thing people should do to heal from their emotional wounds, hurts and imprintings from their past.

My answer was short and direct. Confront and confess whatever it is that is keeping you from changing.

Many people are simply unwilling to open the door of yesterday and see the real problem. Some open it but look through stained glass windows. They can only see the mistakes of others. They live in the blame game. The truth is that the only person anyone can change is themselves.

Change will only come to those who are willing to confront and confess the issue, even if the issue is them!

## LIFE PRINCIPLE
*Confront And Confess Whatever Is Keeping You From Changing.*

You only get one life. You don't get two or three chances to win. What is keeping you from living life to its fullest? What is keeping you from seizing your day and walking free from the prison of your past, your pain and your hurt? ***You only have one life. Live it to win!***

Confront whatever it is. Confronting means

that you are no longer lying to yourself; you're willing to stand up and expose everything that is keeping you from changing. The enemy that has held you for so many years must be met head on. No more fear. No more worrying about what others may think or say. Stand up and confront to win.

The enemy you fail to face and conquer does not only affect your life, but the lives of those around you. Stand up, fight Hell and win this war in your present so that your wounds and weaknesses do not bleed into the lives of others.

## LIFE PRINCIPLE
*Sweat The Small Stuff... Little Problems Can Become Big Ones When They Grow Up!*

Life will always be stressful if you don't make a commitment to face and fight all the enemies that are trying to defeat you. I don't just mean people who leave you or talk about you. They are not the enemy; they are being used by your enemy. I want to identify what I believe are some of your most dangerous adversaries, and it's not just the devil.

I once read a book entitled, "Don't Sweat the Small Stuff." I was thinking about that phrase when all of a sudden this inner voice says to me, *"No, you better sweat the small stuff."* It was the little things in King Solomon's life that cost him a great deal. The little weaknesses became huge problems at the end of his life.

David ignored his weakness and it almost cost him the kingdom. Samson ignored his weakness and it cost him everything.

Samson was anointed at birth to be a deliverer to his people, the Israelites. He was dedicated as a Nazarene unto God. Samson wasn't supposed to drink strong drink, enter into marriages with women from other nations or cut his hair.

Just because you're anointed for purpose doesn't mean you don't have any weaknesses. Samson refused to address, face and conquer his. ***Never make peace with a weakness... it will win in the end***. We have the power through Jesus Christ and the Holy Spirit to conquer our weaknesses when we stop hiding them and expose them to the light. Jesus is made strong in our weaknesses (II Corinthians 12:9). The number one enemy to your success isn't the devil or anyone around you. The number one enemy to your success **is you!**

Go after your weaknesses; they are the key Hell will use to lure you to your demise. Satan's goal is not to physically kill you, but to kill your purpose and your anointing.

## LIFE PRINCIPLE
***Your Greatest Adversary Isn't The Devil...
Your Greatest Adversary Is You!***

Find out who the enemy is using to feed your weakness and swiftly move... run and don't look back!

*"The rulers of the Philistines went to her and said, "See if you can lure him into showing you the secret of his great strength and how we can overpower him so we may tie him up and subdue him. Each one of us will give you eleven hundred shekels..."* Judges 16:5 NIV

In this story, the enemy used a beautiful woman named Delilah to discover Samson's weakness. Delilah stayed around long enough to break Samson's focus. If Samson would have worked the life principle that confusion is proof a deceiver could be present, he may have started looking more closely at the people around him. He would have discovered that Delilah wasn't a friend but a foe. She was a predator sent by the enemy to blind him, destroy him and rob him of his anointing. They wanted to lure Samson, not to kill him, but rob him of his purpose.

## LIFE PRINCIPLE
### *Never Trivialize Your Weaknesses.*

Samson's weakness caused him to reveal the secret to his strength which was in his hair. Samson was anointed to deliver the people of God from the Philistines. Because he did not deal with his weakness, he gave his enemy strength.

The enemy shaved his head, plucked out his eyes and bound him to a grinder's wheel. This must have weighed heavy in Samson's mind. Think for a moment. Samson was blind but could hear the laughs of the enemy taunting, *"Samson, here we are. Come and kill us... Samson, where is your precious God?"*

Every day he had to be reminded of his weakness by the enemy he was destined to destroy. However, the enemy failed to notice Samson's hair growing back. Samson's strength returned, and God used what the enemy overlooked to defeat them.

*"Then Samson prayed to the LORD, "O Sovereign LORD, remember me. O God, please strengthen me just once more, and let me with one blow get revenge on the Philistines for my two eyes." Then Samson reached toward the two central pillars on which the temple stood. Bracing himself against them, his right hand on the one and his left hand on the other...Then*

*he pushed with all his might, and down came the temple on the rulers and all the people in it. Thus he killed many more when he died than while he lived."* Judges 16:28-30

**When the enemy has counted you out...God has counted you in!** Don't stay bound to the mistakes of yesterday. God is able to restore you even when it looks like there is no hope for tomorrow. It doesn't matter how much the enemy has stolen. There is something left inside of you that is enough to get you to your destiny!

## CHAPTER FIVE

# THE ROOT WILL ALWAYS PRODUCE THE FRUIT

*N*o good tree bears bad fruit, nor does a bad tree bear good fruit. Each tree is recognized by its own fruit. People do not pick figs from thorn bushes, or grapes from briers. The good man brings good things out of the good stored up in his heart, and the evil man brings evil things out of the evil stored up in his heart. For out of the overflow of his heart his mouth speaks." Luke 6:43-45 NIV

Have you ever noticed people who are always in the same rut? Maybe you are one of those people who always seem to be in the same place in life.

Changing things around you doesn't mean you're changed. Let's say you have an attitude problem at your job. You go to work and have problems everyday with your co-workers and even your boss. You begin to hate your job and start blaming the problem on people around you.

## LIFE PRINCIPLE
*Changing Things Around You Doesn't Mean You are Changing...All You've Done Is Rearrange The Furniture.*

What do you do? Do you examine yourself for wrong behavior? No, you start looking for another job. In this cycle, you keep moving from one job to another and find yourself in the same place every time, having problems with your co-workers and boss.

The problem isn't the people around you. The problem is the fruit you are producing in your life.

That fruit is produced by the root of something deeper in you. If you are always looking at situations and people around you, you will never find peace in your life. The root always produces the fruit.

If you keep finding yourself eating the same fruit in life, even after you have made changes, you need to examine your root. The soil doesn't decide what the seed is. The soil reveals what the seed is to become.

The soil is the thing around us that force what we really are, to be revealed. These things are usually crises that have surrounded our lives. Crises are a normal part of life. Crisis will force change. Most of us wouldn't be who we are right now if we hadn't experienced crisis. It was the crisis around us that forced us to look for a way out. The soil unlocks the root, the root reveals the tree and the tree at maturity reveals the fruit.

## LIFE PRINCIPLE
*The Soil Doesn't Decide What The Seed Is;*
*The Soil Reveals What The Seed Is.*

What fruit are others eating from your life? Circumstances don't make us, they reveal us. When does the olive become the oil? The olive becomes the oil after it has been pressed beyond recognition. When the pressure around the olive becomes too unbearable, it forces the outward shell of the olive to surrender to what has been placed inside of it. The olive as we know it ceases to exist and becomes something even greater. It becomes the oil. ***Anything we are becoming is by the result of pressure.***

In the movie "The Devil's Advocate", the devil was interviewing a lawyer for hire. The devil says to this successful lawyer who had never lost a case, "*I don't care how many cases you've won. Pressure; that's what I want to know. How do you perform under pressure? You will either fold or focus under pressure. Anyone can win when there is no pressure, but can you win when you are under extreme pressure?*"

Pressure is what the soil produces to force the seed to reveal what is inside. Crisis, pain, trials, tribulations, heartache and wounds are the pressure. This is the soil that forces what we are, to be revealed.

Stop trying to trim the hedge. Stop trying to clean up the surface. You can't fix the fruit until you deal with the root. The root is hidden in a place that no one else can see. It's the root of a man that decides what he is becoming and what he is doing.

*"Seeing in the distance a fig tree in leaf, he went to find out if it had any fruit. When he reached it, he found nothing but leaves, because it was not the season for figs. Then he said to the tree, "May no one ever eat fruit from you again." And his disciples heard him say it."* Mark 11:13-14 NIV

Jesus was hungry and saw a fig tree with leaves on it which was a sign that the tree was fruitful. When Jesus lifted up the leaves to take of the fruit, He found the tree empty. Jesus became angry because the tree promoted maturity on the surface but in reality it produced no fruit.

This story reminds me of what a lot of people in the church look like. We have become masters at surface Christianity. We have learned how to use "leaves" to give the appearance of fruitfulness and maturity; however, when people come to us hungry and in need, they discover a tree bearing no fruit.

Notice how Jesus responds to this false appearance. *"May no one ever eat fruit from you again."* The next season that tree was dead, all the way to the root.

I pray for you, as I pray for myself. Let's stop this surface living, attack the root of our problems and kill those things in our lives that are hindering us from good fruit.

*"The ax is already at the root of the trees, and every tree that does not produce good fruit will be cut down and thrown into the fire."* Luke 3:9 NIV

Let's deal with it now so that God doesn't have to throw us into the fire. Remember the verse in the opening of this chapter. No good tree produces bad fruit and no bad tree produces good fruit. The fruit is a portrait of the root.

## THERE IS A DIFFERENCE BETWEEN SOMEONE BEING SENT AND SOMEONE THAT JUST WENT.

If you have a bad root system, you are unable to be corrected. You will not be able to change unless you allow someone to point out your pain, wounds and weaknesses. If you are not willing to be pruned, or corrected, the words that should promote you will offend you. Many people leave without being sent when they should plant themselves and grow a better root system.

Our churches are full of people who went instead of being sent. The root system in their lives has caused them to keep eating the same fruit and they have found themselves even further off course. You will experience a peace-filled life when you learn how to be sent by God and those He has placed in authority.

Ever wonder why some people keep repeating the same realities? They can move from one state to another but within months are right back in the same situation. They go from one bad relationship to another instead of learning and growing from them. The faces have changed but the fruit is the same. You must be willing to allow someone to expose the rotten root system if you want to produce healthy fruit!

There is a misconception that we are not supposed to judge people's fruit? The truth is we are all supposed to be fruit inspectors.

The fruit reveals the root. Take the time in your prayer life to open your eyes and see the real you. Stop the blame game. Stop using excuses.

In most cases the problem is you! You are the only person who can fix you! Start focusing on your root. Take a good, hard look at your flaws and weaknesses and confess them to God. Dig up all those bad roots. Allow God to heal you and plant new seeds for your next season.

# CHAPTER SIX

# PLACE A HIGHER VALUE
# ON YOUR FAMILY

*S*omeone once said, "You can be the poorest person on the earth but if you have a strong family you are rich..." I don't care how poor a man is; if he has his family he is rich.

The three major institutions in our country are the home, the church and the state. The home is the oldest and most sacred of all institutions.

When God decided to create man, He realized it wasn't good for him to be alone. The gift of a wife was God's greatest gift to Adam. She was not made from his head to be ruled by him, nor from his heel that he might trample on her. God made her from his side so she could own and command his love. She was his equal because she was a part of him.

## LIFE PRINCIPLE
*The Family Is A Haven In A Heartless World.*

**Family is important to God!** God gave Adam and Eve the ability to produce and create a family. The family is one of God's masterpieces.

**FIVE AREAS TO WORK ON TO KEEP YOUR FAMILY TOGETHER:**

1. THE FAMILY TABLE

The family dinner table has become a forgotten art of communication and love. My family eats dinner together several nights a week and find ourselves laughing and joking as we talk about the day. I have found that some of our best times together have taken place sitting around the dinner table just talking. Build your family around the table. I've realized that this time is a very important process in keeping and growing the family.

> ## LIFE PRINCIPLE
> *"The Only Rock I Know That Stays Steady, The Only Institution I Know That Works Is The Family." Lee Iacocca*

## 2. FAMILY ACTIVITIES

Take vacations! Take days and spend it with your whole family. Make time to grow together. I have found that this is a great way to get to know your children.

Dr. Mike Murdock said to me one day, *"Son, don't become so big that you can't enjoy your life."* These have been strong and helpful words of mentorship. I would rather grow my kids before I grow my ministry.

## 3. CHILDREN'S ACTIVITES

I can't believe how many parents don't go and support their children in extra-curricular activities.

My son once competed in a wrestling tournament that lasted ALL DAY LONG! We waited for him to wrestle a six minute match and then waited hours for his next match to begin. At the end of the day he was wrestling for the gold medal. His opponent was a good friend of his and neither wanted to wrestle each other. My son lost the match by one point and all of us were hurting for his loss. My son had so many of his family present to cheer him in his wins and comfort him in his losses.

After the crowds had faded, we were walking out of the arena. I walked by the boy who had won the gold medal. Walking over to congratulate him, he looked up and immediately asked how my son was doing. I replied, *"Fine, but don't worry about him, this is your victory. Enjoy it."* As I walked away, I turned to see a young boy rubbing his Gold Medal all by himself. There was no one, not one family member there all day to celebrate his victory.

He came by himself, performed and won by himself, got on the bus and probably went home to a house that was empty and cold. Where was his dad? Where was his mom? Someone tell me what's going to happen to this country if we don't stand up and build our kids?

I don't care how much you need to build your business. Take time to build your kids. Let them look around and see your face watching them in the crowd.

## LIFE PRINCIPLE
*Mothers Decide What Children Believe;*
*Fathers Decide What They Remember.*

4. THE FAMILY ALTAR

Take your kids to church. Stop pointing the way and lead the way. Establish their need for God.

I pastor a church in Hickory, North Carolina called The Favor Center. Many times I watch our youth come into service all by themselves. When I ask them how they got to church they tell me they had to beg their mother or father to bring me. Parents stop pointing the way and start leading the way!

5. REMEMBER SHE WAS YOUR WIFE BEFORE SHE BECAME A MOTHER; HE WAS YOUR HUSBAND BEFORE HE BECAME A FATHER.

It is important to keep the romance alive in your marriage. Take a date night each week. Tell your spouse you love them every day. Remember what it was like before you had children. Keep the flame alive!

I wrote a book that discusses more on the subject of the family. You can order this book entitled *"Survive to Thrive"* on my website @ www.godstrongtv.com.

# CHAPTER SEVEN

# CULTIVATE A POSITIVE MIND

*"You will keep him in perfect peace, whose mind is stayed on You, because he trusts in You."* Isaiah 26:3 NKJV

We need to learn how to follow our peace. In this world of fast food, fast cars and fast living, we have lost the ability to slow down and extract what's been engrafted in our day. Think about it; we use to cook on the stove. Now, we have become a people of the microwave. I have stood by the microwave having a fit because a minute wasn't fast enough to cook my food. Can you believe it? What use to take at least ten minutes to cook can now be cooked in one minute in the microwave oven. Now we become agitated when a minute is not fast enough to satisfy our desire.

## LIFE PRINCIPLE
### *Slow Down Before You Blow Up.*

How can we find peace in this *"fast paced, busy, get to where you're going and back"* world?

Remember how slow the internet was when it first started? It didn't matter because we didn't know it could be faster. Now we have high speed internet and become irritated and frustrated when we are forced to endure a dial up connection. I believe we have lost the ability to wait and enjoy what's happening in a moment. Most of us are already planning the next moment before we can enjoy and extract from the moment we are presently in.

- Suicide is at an all time high.
- Depression is off the chart.
- Stress is killing the American family.
- Bitterness is weighing us down.
- The inability to wait is causing us to fall in a trap of debt and credit problems.
- Hatred for others is forcing us to become cynical and critical to truth.

If we don't slow down and change, we are going to destroy the only life we have. You have one life to live; let's decide to live it to the fullest.

We weren't promised a second life. You are only given one opportunity to run this race. Once this body dies, it's dead.

Do you want peace? Decide right now to stop all the stress and worry. Open your eyes and learn to see what God has engrafted in your days. Days are made up of many moments.

The word moment is defined as, *"a definite point in time or in a series of events; an indefinitely brief period of time; instant."* Moments on top of each other create what we call a day. Days become weeks, weeks become months and months become years. The reality is that they all started as moments.

I've often wondered how many moments I have wasted. How many times have I let a bad moment ruin a good day with my children, my wife and family? Think how easy it is to allow one little thing to spoil the whole loaf of our lives.

*"A little leaven leavens the whole lump."* Galatians 5:9-10 NKJV

If we want a peaceful mind we must do what Isaiah instructed; keep our mind on Him.

## LIFE PRINCIPLE
### *There Are No Bad Days Only Bad Moments.*

Keep your focus on the Lord instead of what you are going through. This invokes the power of trust. Jesus said many times not to allow the cares of this life to cause us stress. He told us not to worry! Don't become so focused on what you do not have, that you fail to see what you do have.

*"Then Jesus said to his disciples: "Therefore I tell you, **do not worry about your life**, what you will eat; or about your body, what you will wear. Life is more than food, and the body more than clothes."* Luke 12:22-23 NIV

- *Worry is confidence in the adversary.*
- *Worry is proof you lack the faith to believe it can be better.*
- *Worry is the complete opposite of faith.*
- *Worry can create seasons of sickness.*
- *Worry proves what the enemy has placed on you is working.*
- *Worry could cancel out what God has sent to bless you.*

Do you worry a lot? Are you always stressed out about something in your life? When your mind is consumed with so much worry, it is impossible to hear from God. When we stop hearing, our faith stops growing. Without faith we will be stuck in our present season for a long time.

I will tell you a great secret that I recently discovered about walking in a peaceful mind. It may go against religious thinking but trust me, it works.

One of my good friends got to sit down with one of the "Generals" in the Body of Christ, Dr. Oral Roberts. Dr. Roberts instructed him to learn and understand Luke 10:2.

*"Then He said to them, "The harvest truly is great, but the laborers are few; therefore pray **the Lord of the harvest** to send out laborers into His harvest. Go your way; behold, I send you out as lambs among wolves."* Luke 10:2-3 NKJV

When we sow our seeds in obedience we position ourselves under open heavens. Your increase is not in the hand of the enemy, nor is it in the hands of the people. You can rest with peace when you release your seed to advance the Kingdom because you have activated God, the Lord of the harvest.

*"The **harvest is plentiful** but the workers are few. Ask the **Lord of the harvest**, therefore, to send out workers into his harvest field."* Matthew 9:37-38 NIV

The word harvest is the key I want to focus on in this passage. God is the Lord of those who advance His Kingdom.

The word harvest is defined as *a supply of anything gathered at maturity and stored; the result or consequence of any act, process, or event.*

In Luke, Jesus refers to God as the Lord of the harvest. If God is the Lord of the harvest, then someone has to be lord of the seed.

*"They will wage war against the Lamb, but the Lamb will triumph over them because he is **Lord of lords and King of kings** — and with him will be his called, chosen and faithful followers."* Revelation 17:14 NIV

## LIFE PRINCIPLE
### *Admit That God Is Your Source.*

The Word of God declares that Jesus is Lord of lords (lower case letter l) and King of kings (lower case letter k). King refers to ruler ship. Lord refers to ownership. We are the landlords of this earth. We govern His affairs.

What are we lords of? Not the earth, because the earth is God's and the substance thereof (Psalms 24:1). Therefore, we are the **lords of the seed.** We only have power over our seed. What we are willing to let go of allows God, the Lord of the harvest, to be activated over our lives.

This surely does produce a peaceful mind. Do what you can; God will do what you can't.

**Follow your peace!** Stop making your job, your boss and the people around you your source. You may work for someone, but ultimately it is God who allows the increase in your life to be released. He is the Lord of the harvest. He is your source.

Remember the Lord your God, for it is He who gives you the power to get wealth. God is the source of all power, increase and promotion. This understanding will create in you a life of peace.

# CHAPTER EIGHT

# GOD'S ESCAPE PLAN

*D*ecide to be delivered, not from your

crisis but into your next season.

*"And because the king, in his anger, had demanded such a hot fire in the furnace, the flames killed the soldiers as they threw the three men in. So Shadrach, Meshach, and Abednego, securely tied, fell into the roaring flames."* Daniel 3:22-23 NLT

In reading this story about these three Hebrew young men named Shadrach, Meshach and Abednego, I have discovered something that is very uplifting and encouraging to me. We have been conditioned to believe that we should try and escape our crises instead of facing them.

King Nebuchadnezzar made an image and wanted the people to bow down and worship it. Shadrach, Meshach and Abednego decided not to bow. They were captured, taken to the king and given a chance to change their minds. I love the attitude and resolve of these boys. Look at their response to King Nebuchadnezzar.

*"Shadrach, Meshach, and Abednego replied, "O Nebuchadnezzar, we do not need to defend ourselves before you. If we are thrown into the blazing furnace, the God whom we serve is able to save us. He will rescue us from your power, Your Majesty.* **but even if he doesn't, we want to make it clear to you, Your Majesty, that we will never serve your**

*gods or worship the gold statue you have set up.*" Daniel 3:16-18 NLT

I love the way they stood up to their crisis. They showed a resolve and faith in their belief and what was right. Their belief in God outweighed their fear of death. Even if God didn't deliver them, they knew He was still worthy.

## STOP TRYING TO WALK AWAY FROM, AND LEARN HOW TO WALK INTO.

You can't frustrate someone who has the mind set to stand no matter what, praise no matter what, worship no matter what and give no matter what!

How do we act? Do we offer up praise and faith only when God responds in our favor? What if God doesn't respond in our timing? Could you still praise Him? Could you stand for God even if He didn't respond?

These boys were convinced that God is worth standing for, not because of what He is doing or what He does, but because of who He is! He is God! He's the one true source of greatness on the earth. Let me inform you in case you don't know this... God is God all by himself. He doesn't need us to confirm that He is.

## LIFE PRINCIPLE
*Endurance Is A Qualifier... Never Give In... Never Give Up... God Will Come Through In The End!*

This angered King Nebuchadnezzar so much that he turned up the furnace seven times hotter. Their crisis just increased. Wait a minute! Shouldn't

God have shown up by now? Maybe He had. Maybe God was already there and waiting to see if the boys would discern that the crisis was meant to go through and not be rescued from.

The fire was so hot it killed the guards that were assigned to throw them in. They were standing at the mouth of the furnace with no enemy present to throw them in.

Many of us would have assumed that this was God's deliverance; that God was freeing us from our enemy. However, Shadrach, Meshach and Abednego were still bound hand and foot. This is not true freedom.

Many Christians believe that they are free but have misinterpreted the events around them. Instead of going through the crisis, they try to walk away from the crisis and are still bound by the enemy.

*"We will never serve or worship your God. Even if God does not deliver us..."* This is awesome! This is what it takes to overcome the enemy. A mind of real worship is to stay connected and devoted even while heaven appears shut. When you stand, Heaven will eventually open and you will be blessed beyond measure.

*"And these three men, Shadrach, Meshach, and Abednego, fell down bound into the midst of the burning fiery furnace."* Daniel 3:23 NKJV

These three boys threw themselves into the fire. I can't believe that they didn't try to escape. God's escape plan is always different than what we would think as a way out. His way out seems to always be going in and through. They fell into the fire and stepped into their problem. This is where the mind of the real believer begins to show itself. They wanted to be where God's purpose was. It wasn't about them.

The truth is it is never about us. It has always been about God and His purpose. When we understand this law we will handle our crisis better.

## LIFE PRINCIPLE
*God's Presence Is The Only Place Where Your Weaknesses Will Die.*

When they entered the fire they actually entered into the very presence of God. In God's presence our bondage is loosed. It's only in His presence that our weaknesses die. When is the last time you lingered in His presence until your weaknesses died? This is real dedication and real worship. This is one of the only ways to show your love for His purpose.

*"Then King Nebuchadnezzar was astonished; and he rose in haste and spoke, saying to his counselors, 'Did we not cast three men bound into the midst of the fire?' They answered and said to the king, 'True, O king.' 'Look!' he answered, 'I see four men loose, walking in the midst of the fire; and they are not hurt, and the form of the fourth is like the Son of God'."* Daniel 3:24-25 NKJV

The king was astonished and amazed. There was a fourth man in the fire whose appearance was like the son of God. The quickest place to have an encounter or visitation of this magnitude is to place yourself in a position that forces God to react to your faith. Their willingness to stand caused heaven to react on their behalf. God's purpose wasn't just to deliver them from the furnace but to deliver everyone else around the furnace. Their commitment to stand not only saved them but also those who were watching, including the one who sentenced them to die.

*"Then Nebuchadnezzar went near the mouth of the burning fiery furnace and spoke, saying, 'Shadrach, Meshach, and Abednego, servants of the Most High God, come out, and come here'..."* Daniel 3:26 NKJV

Doesn't this seem crazy? The door of the furnace opened but they wouldn't leave until the king called for them. This is the place I want to be in my walk with God. I want to be so in tune with God and His presence that even when the door to my crisis has opened I won't leave. I will stay as long as the Spirit is in the fire with me. I will have to be summoned. How about you? Wouldn't you like to have that kind of faith, the kind of faith that doesn't waver even in the worst crisis?

It's all about God's will and God's purpose. Jesus knew this, Paul knew this and the Old Testament Patriarchs knew this. Those who didn't usually failed and suffered greatly.

## LIFE PRINCIPLE
*Your Reaction Speaks Louder To God Than Your Praise.*

**Can God trust you?** Think about it before you answer. Can God really trust you? What if He allowed you to go through what Paul and Silas went through in Acts 16? They were arrested, beaten, thrown into jail and shackled, all so that the jailer and his family might come to know the Lord.

I preach all the time about reactions. Everything in your life is about a reaction. I ask you again, can God trust you? Can He trust you to go through the fire, through the pain and through the circumstances without being offended, upset or saying things that give Him a bad name? Can you stand no matter what? If you can, get ready for a move of God on your behalf! Remember, it is always about His purpose and not yours.

**"Nobody ever did, or ever will, escape the consequences of his choices." Alfred A. Montapert**

*"...Then Shadrach, Meshach, and Abednego came from the midst of the fire. And the satraps, administrators, governors, and the king's counselors gathered together, and they saw these men on whose bodies the fire had no power; the hair of their head was not singed nor were their garments affected, and the smell of fire was not on them. Nebuchadnezzar spoke, saying, 'Blessed be the God of Shadrach, Meshach, and Abed-Nego, who sent His Angel and delivered His servants who trusted in Him, and they have frustrated the king's word, and yielded their bodies, that they should not serve nor worship any god except their own God! Therefore I make a decree that any people, nation, or language which speaks anything amiss against the God of Shadrach, Meshach, and Abednego shall be cut in pieces, and their houses shall be made an ash heap; because there is no other God who can deliver like this'."* Daniel 3:26-29 NKJV

Their reactions to the purpose of God and what was right brought salvation to Babylon. It was God's purpose to reach King Nebuchadnezzar. Their reaction changed the king's reaction; he became their defender instead of their punisher. If anyone spoke wrong about their God, He had them killed. Shadrach, Meshach and Abednego made it about God's purpose and will. Let me encourage you; you will not be left wanting when you put God first.

*"Then the king* **promoted** *Shadrach, Meshach, and Abednego in the province of Babylon."* Daniel 3:30 NKJV

## CHAPTER NINE

# THE MIND IGNORES THE FAMILIAR

Dr. Jerry A. Grillo

*"I, the Lord, search the heart; I test the mind, even to give every man according to his ways, according to the fruit of his doings."* Jeremiah 17:10 NKJV

The greatest key you will learn is that your mind is the tool to all you know and all you can be. I have said it more than once in my life. Your mind is your world. If you don't gain any other understanding you must gain this one key. Your mind decides more than you give it credit for. Our mind decides our feelings, our offences and our level of faith. It is in the mind where you decide the quality of life. Your mind is a garden; you decide whether weeds or flowers grow there.

I have often wondered why so many in our churches are still stuck in the same rut. Why do people seem to fight the same demons for years? After observing the habits of most people, I have come to this conclusion. Most people give more attention to the outward appearance of the flesh then they give to cultivating their minds.

One of the reasons we have so many problems in our marriages, homes and churches is that the mind becomes familiar with what is important and begins to ignore what needs to be recognized and embraced.

The word familiar can also be defined as common, well known, often encountered or ordinary. This happens when we stay around someone for any length of time. How we act and treat people in the beginning isn't usually how we treat them after we get to know them. We do this in all kinds of relationships.

This one key is the reason marriages suffer. Spouses that once catered to one another's needs, begin to ignore those same needs over time. They lose the passion to pursue one another because they have become familiar with one another.

Most Christians live on their first encounter they had with the Lord. They can't move past their confession of faith to grow and become fully mature in Him. I've seen it even in my own walk. In the first season of my salvation, if anyone talked about the Lord I would become teary eyed and have this uncontrollable urge to lift my hands and praise God. You were probably the same way. There was such a hunger to read God's word. As a matter of fact, the first purchase I made after I received Jesus as my Savior was a New American Standard Bible. I would get up early to pray and go to all kinds of places to hear the preaching and teaching of God's word. I decided not to go on my senior trip with unsaved classmates. I went to a Christian conference that had the appearance of "WoodStock".

Imagine thousands of youth and adults sleeping and having services in a big field. The Lord personally called me for full time ministry at this conference. What a hunger I had! Now, thirty years later I have to fight to stay focused, to pray and to even study my Bible. What has happened? What the mind becomes familiar with, the mind decides to take for granted and ignore.

*"I beseech you therefore, brethren, by the mercies of God, that you present your bodies a living sacrifice, holy, acceptable to God, which is your reasonable*

*service. And do not be conformed to this world, but be transformed by the **renewing of your mind**, that you may prove what is that good and acceptable and perfect will of God."* Romans 12:1-2 NKJV

We are instructed not to conform but be transformed. This transformation happens by renewing our minds. The word conformed means to get stuck in a pattern. You must fight the desire to live in a rut. Your mind becomes bored, stops thinking and feeling challenged when you live in a rut.

## LIFE PRINCIPLE
### *Your Mind Is Your World.*

Refuse to become religious in your walk with God. Time has a way of getting the best of us. Many have allowed time to rob them of their zeal and distract them from their goals. Decide today to use time to grow, mature and develop a more powerful mindset. Don't just exist...LIVE!

The word 'transformed' comes from the Greek word "metamorphoo" from where we get the word metamorphous. Metamorphous means *to change in form, or nature: transform; subject to or undergo metamorphosis; marked or complete change of character, appearance and condition, etc.*

Our minds are to be transformed daily. The mind is your intellect, feelings and will. We have to control what the mind tries to become familiar with. We decide what stays new in our minds which keeps our emotions and will at a healthy desire.

I have to decide every day that my family, my ministry and my God will not become so familiar to me that I begin to ignore them.

## LAW OF RECOGNITION

One of the greatest books I've ever read is by Dr. Mike Murdock. In his book "The Law of Recognition", he says anything unrecognized will go unnoticed and unrewarded and will eventually exit your life. The key to a long and lasting relationship is hidden in the law of recognition. What we become familiar with we ignore. If we ignore our spouses, they will eventually exit our lives. If we ignore our children, we will eventually lose them to others. When we ignore our mentors, we eventually become critical and skeptical to their instructions. When we begin to take the Lord and His work for granted and become familiar with His presence, we will lose access to Him. Our worship, passion, love, giving, pursuit and focus will change. One day we will wake up only to discover that the spirit of the Lord has departed.

This will cause peace to leave us. Our life will become a garden of weeds where there were once flowers. You decide what is planted in your garden; not your enemy.

Who have you become familiar with? Repent right now and begin to seek the Lord for healing and renewal so that you will not lose their love and connection. Do it before you wake up and find yourself alone.

---

### LIFE PRINCIPLE
*"Anything Unrecognized Will Exit Your Life." Mike Murdock*

---

- *Recognition decides access.*

- *Recognition decides longevity to a relationship.*
- *Recognition decides the level of your worship and praise.*
- *Recognition allows a relationship to grow deeper.*
- *Recognition helps others feel good about themselves.*

Stop ignoring what is important! Rule your mind or it will rule you.

Dr. Jerry A. Grillo

## CHAPTER TEN

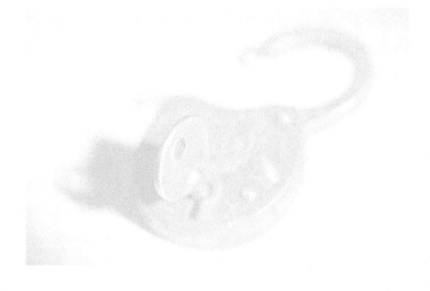

# EMBRACE AND CULTIVATE YOUR DREAMS

*T*he greatest gift we have in life is the ability to dream of our future and what we want to be.

- *A dream is the only way to leave your present and enter your future.*
- *A dream cost you nothing except using your imagination.*

Make your dreams bigger than you, and God will get involved. Develop a dream you can't afford, and it will pull others into it. The beauty about dreaming is that you can enter a whole new world without leaving your present.

**FACTS ABOUT DREAMS:**
1. Dreams give you focus for the future.
2. A dream creates hope for tomorrow.
3. A dream is the first process of creating a goal.
4. Those who don't dream are stuck in their present.
5. A dream decides your level of excitement.

## LIFE PRINCIPLE
*A Dream Makes Life Bearable.*

God will give you a dream, but He will never show you the journey. God gave Joseph a dream of his future, but He didn't show him the journey it would take to get there. Most of us wouldn't believe in the dream if God showed us the pit falls and problems we would have to survive for the dream to become a reality. However, without the dream the pit falls and valleys in life may stop us from believing in our future. Thus without dreams we would give up and die. Think for a moment what Joseph might have done if he had no dream of his future when his brothers threw him in a dried up well and was sold into slavery.

## LIFE PRINCIPLE
*God Will Always Show You The Future; He Rarely Shows You The Journey.*

How did Joseph survive his pain?

1. **He never discussed his pain or problems.** He never talked about his brothers while serving in Potiphar's house. He never discussed Potiphar's wife after being falsely accused and surviving a season in prison. He never talked about being a prisoner when he was in Pharaoh's presence.

2. **He wasn't a complainer.** He didn't complain about his problems or plight. He became second in command in Egypt, and when his brothers showed up he told them, *"What you meant for harm, my God turned for good!"* He kept this attitude throughout his journey and never allowed his crisis to change his focus.

3. **He never stopped believing in the dream.**
   He stayed committed to the promise of his dream.

That's how we must live to win. We must stay committed to the dream that God has given us no matter what. Set goals and deadlines, never discussing the pain but always talking about the dream. **Speak it... build it... believe it... and it will come**.

> ## LIFE PRINCIPLE
> *A Goal Is A Dream With A Deadline.*

Don't be afraid to dream big and do great things. There is a false doctrine filtrating through our churches that we should not expect or believe for more. This is a lie and a gospel of false humility based on the scripture in 1 Timothy that has been completely misinterpreted.

*"And having food and clothing, with these we shall be content. But those who desire to be rich fall into temptation and a snare, and into many foolish and harmful lusts which drown men in destruction and perdition. For the love of money is a root of all kinds of evil, for which some have strayed from the faith in their greediness, and pierced themselves through with many sorrows."* 1 Timothy 6:8-10 NKJV

Let me show the translation of this scripture in the Message Bible.

*"If we have bread on the table and shoes on our feet, that's enough. But if it's only money these leaders are after, they'll self-destruct in no time. Lust for money brings trouble and nothing but trouble. Going down that path, some lose their footing in the faith completely and live to regret it bitterly ever after."* 1Timothy 6:8-10 THE MESSAGE

If you study these scriptures you will discover that Paul was teaching Timothy to be content, not satisfied. The word content means to be happy no matter what situation or circumstance you are in.

Things should not define us. Material gain or loss shouldn't make or break us. We are called to be Disciples of Christ and to do the work of the ministry regardless of our financial status.

Paul was not telling Timothy that being prosperous is evil. I know wealthy people who are completely on fire for God. Having more and wanting more is not evil. Money is not evil... loving money is. Jesus is my focus and the center of all I do, but make no mistake about it; I need more money. It takes money to do to the work of the ministry. This very book in your hands wouldn't have been published unless there were finances available to do it.

So many churches are preaching a gospel of death and not the gospel of life. John 10:10 tells us that Jesus came to give us a more abundant life!

I spoke with a man one time who had called me. He was very angry and rebuking me because I teach that people should desire more. He asked me what I believed that he deserved in life. I told him that he deserved life, God's best, to be healed and to be prosperous.

He raised his voice and said, "No! I deserve death!" I could hardly believe my ears. I immediately replied, "I rebuke that! You don't deserve death." God didn't send Jesus because we deserve death; He sent him because we deserve to live!

Do you want to live to win? Then you better dream you're a winner. Run from people who are walking in false humility. They are a danger to the Kingdom of God. Jesus had to deal with this same attitude and in the end they were the ones screaming,

"Kill Him! Crucify Him!"

This is not the real gospel but a man-made religious idea. This mindset births complacency and stops people from growing and striving to become better. Change is not the focus and people with this belief system will live their lives broke, sick, mean, angry and bitter.

It is crazy to believe that God doesn't desire us to increase and produce more. Look at the following story in the Gospel of Matthew:

*"Again, it will be like a man going on a journey, who called his servants and entrusted his wealth to them. To one he gave five bags of gold, to another two bags, and to another one bag, each according to his ability. Then he went on his journey. The man who had received five bags of gold went at once and put his money to work and gained five bags more. So also, the one with the two bags of gold gained two more. But the man who had received one bag went off, dug a hole in the ground and hid his master's money. After a long time the master of those servants returned and settled accounts with them. The man who had received five bags of gold brought the other five. 'Master,' he said, 'you entrusted me with five bags of gold. See, I have gained five more. His master replied, 'Well done, good and faithful servant! You have been faithful with a few things; I will put you in charge of many things. Come and share your master's happiness!' The man with the two bags of gold also came. 'Master,' he said, 'you entrusted me with two bags of gold; see, I have gained two more. 'His master replied, 'Well done, good and faithful servant! You have been faithful with a few things; I will put you in charge of many things. Come and share your master's happiness!' Then the man who*

*had received one bag of gold came. 'Master,' he said, 'I knew that you are a hard man, harvesting where you have not sown and gathering where you have not scattered seed. So I was afraid and went out and hid your gold in the ground. See, here is what belongs to you.' His master replied, 'You wicked, lazy servant! So you knew that I harvest where I have not sown and gather where I have not scattered seed? Well then, you should have put my money on deposit with the bankers, so that when I returned I would have received it back with interest. So take the bag of gold from him and give it to the one who has ten bags. For whoever who has will be given more, and they will have an abundance. Whoever does not have, even what they have will be taken from them. And throw that worthless servant outside, into the darkness, where there will be weeping and gnashing of teeth."* Matthew 25:14-30 NIV

The whole gospel of Jesus was to multiply and increase. The first command to mankind was to multiply, subdue and have dominion (Genesis 1:28).

I want to **<u>LIVE TO WIN!</u>**

- **Dream big.**
- **Dream often.**
- **Set goals to do and become more.**

You deserve God's best. Your dreams will never be bigger than God's plans for you. Your dreams never make God nervous. Prepare to be great and do great things.

I like the phrase, "A goal is not a dream". A dream is the doorway by which a goal travels through.

You can't set goals until you have a dream. A dream is a vision. A dream is where faith is born and hope survives. Only four percent of the people in the world have a written goal. Could this mean that the other ninety-six percent of the world's population doesn't dream about their future? This thought saddens me because as children we are all full of dreams. Somewhere along the journey, too many people stop believing that their dreams can become a reality.

Take the time right now to write down your dreams. What do you want to be? What do you want to do? If money or time wasn't an option what would you attempt? Stop listening to doomsayers.

## LIFE PRINCIPLE
*A Dream Is The Doorway That Goals Travel Through.*

**Dreams do come true**! Don't ever forget it! When I think of dreams, my mind goes back to a movie I saw years ago about a young boy named Rudy Ruettiger, who dreamed of playing college football for Notre Dame!

Rudy was one of fourteen children growing up in Illinois. As a young boy, Rudy believed if you had a dream you could do anything and be anything. He set his dream on playing football for Notre Dame.

He was not born into a wealthy home; his father had to work three jobs to make ends meet. Rudy also had a learning disability called dyslexia. He was only five foot six, weighed one hundred sixty-five pounds and wasn't fast.

Rudy called himself a dreamer; not a doer! His teachers always ridiculed him, *"Rudy if you were getting graded for day dreaming you would make an 'A'; however, you are failing this class..."* One of his teachers said, "The *only thing day dreaming does is make you grand in your mind, but not in reality.*"

Rudy was accepted into Notre Dame after being denied three times. He set his focus on playing football. He practiced hard and worked long days just to play on the scout team (a practice squad that played practice games with the varsity team).

On the last game of his senior year, Rudy was allowed to dress out and run on the field with all the varsity team. His dream was about to become a reality. With only twenty-eight seconds left on the clock, Rudy was put in the game.

Rudy sacked the quarterback and had the fans in the stands cheering for him! Rudy is one of only two players in Notre Dame History to be carried off the field by his teammates.

Allow this story to build your confidence and inspire you to believe that dreams can and do come true!

## CHAPTER ELEVEN

# BATTLE IS THE SEED FOR TERRITORY

*L*osing your desire to keep fighting through a season of discouragement can be a dangerous place. The season you are living in will become permanent when you stop fighting for your future.

I heard a man of God make a statement that shot faith back into my heart: ***"Battle Is The Seed For Territory."***

God never talked about the enemy or the battle it would take to enter the Promised Land while the children of Israel were wandering in the wilderness. God only spoke of the provision and blessing that the land would provide. However, God led the children of Israel back into bondage when they refused to fight the enemy to enter the land.

This bondage wasn't one that they could pray their way out of. God become their captor; He became the source that held them in the wilderness. Their unwillingness to fight cost them their lives. They all died in the wilderness because they were unwilling to sow the seed of battle.

The only way you will qualify for your future will be your willingness to stand and fight for your promise!

Battle is your seed for ownership, for control and for reward. Battle is the seed for territory. You will lose the harvest of your dreams if you are unwilling to fight!

Battle is the proof that you believe you belong. If you lose the faith to fight you may lose your faith forever. It's easy to want to give up when all you can see are the giants, mountains, critics, skeptics and doubters in your life.

David was able to enter the palace because he was willing to fight. The entire army hid behind the rock of fear, but David decided to face the giant, change his present and move into his future. He was willing to sow the seed of battle that produced his next season.

There were many who could have entered the palace that day. The only qualification was to face the enemy and be willing to fight. Think how many people you know who are living a meaningless life because they fear change. They won't decide to fight for change. Don't live the life of mediocrity. Live the life of plenty.

Don't let your season of discouragement rob you of your courage to face the giant in your life. The battle you face today is the door to your future tomorrow. **Stand! Fight! Win!**

There were seven nations that God instructed the children of Israel to fight to possess the Promised Land.

*"When the Lord your God brings you into the land which you go to possess, and has cast out many nations before you, the Hittites and the Girgashites and the Amorites and the Canaanites and the Perizzites and the Hivites and the Jebusites, seven nations greater and mightier than you."* Deuteronomy 7:1 NKJV

There were more than seven nations but God only instructed them to fight the seven. God knew that when Israel conquered these nations and gathered their spoils that the other smaller nations would line up with them. I love this! You don't have to fight every enemy in your life, just the ones who will produce the most spoils or blessings.

You can ignore the direction and leading of the Lord and spend most of your life fighting every enemy, or you can follow His direction and not live a life of constant warfare. Fight the few to win the many. Never go to war where there are no spoils for your gain.

Don't engage in an argument just to be right. Sometimes it is better to leave and be silent than to engage in verbal warfare with those who probably won't change anyway. Silence doesn't promote weakness. It takes more courage to stay silent when under attack than it does to engage in an argument.

When you stay silent you actually force your enemy to find someone else to fight. Arguing with someone causes anger to rise in you. Your anger may cause you to say things that put ammunition in your enemy's gun.

## LIFE PRINCIPLE
### *Silence Can't Be Misquoted.*

It's normal to want to defend yourself when someone is attacking you, but don't be blindsided into this kind of warfare. Someone asked Billy Graham how he deals with his critics and his enemies. He answered, *"I never feel the need to explain myself to my enemies, thus I never engage in an argument with them."* Your friends don't require explanation and your enemies would never believe you.

I have to discern what battles to engage in all the time. As a pastor, I deal with people who make false accusations because they have been misled, misinformed or led by their emotions instead of Truth. It would be easy to give these people a piece of my mind; however, this would only create a bigger problem as they could leave my presence and distort and talk about me to everyone they meet. This would do more harm to me and my character than theirs. It is better to let it go. There are no rewards in going to battle with them.

All throughout history you will discover that it takes a spirit of a warrior to have great success. All great leaders understand battle. You can't be afraid to fight if you are going to be a successful leader. The difference between welfare and wealth is warfare. God never intended for His people to live a life battle free. On the contrary, God always intended His people to fight. We are to be warriors and not wimps.

Conflict is a part of life. Battle will be your seed for territory. If you want it, expect to fight for it. You can't sit around claiming increase or territory. This will leave you broke and hopeless in the end. If you want to advance, be successful and have a better life, then stand up and prepare for battle.

Warfare will never totally cease in your life. If you are going to move forward then you must put on your battle gear every day and learn to fight! Remember you only have one life to live! Live it to win!

## LIFE PRINCIPLE
*Anything Uncontested In Your Life Will Flourish.*

*"Finally, my brethren, be strong in the Lord and in the power of His might. Put on the whole armor of God, that you may be able to stand against the wiles of the devil. For we do not wrestle against flesh and blood, but against principalities, against powers, against the rulers of the darkness of this age, against*

*spiritual hosts of wickedness in the heavenly places. Therefore take up the whole armor of God, that you may be able to withstand in the evil day, and having done all, to stand."* Ephesians 6:10-13 NKJV

# CHAPTER TWELVE

# LIFE IS AN OCCASION, RISE TO IT

*L*ife is an event...life is an occasion. Life
was meant to be lived and not resented. So many
people hate their lives. This was never what God
intended. God didn't give us back our life so that we
would hate it but that we would live life more
abundantly (John 10:10).

**You only have one life to live... my prayer is
that you are ready to live it to win!**

"IF" is the law of exchange. Everything in life is based
on 'The Law of If'. The word 'if' is found centered in
the word 'life'. The word 'life' appears four hundred
fifty times and the word 'if' appears one thousand five
hundred ninety-five times in the Bible (KJV).

## LIFE PRINCIPLE
*"IF" Is The Center Of Life... "IF" Is The Door
To The Law Of Exchange.*

Life is full of opportunities. "If" is the hinge
that the door of opportunity swings on. The only
reason so many miss their next season is their failure
to see the opportunity when it appears. This is
because opportunity almost always masks itself in a
problem, a storm or a crisis. Most people only see the
problem, crisis and storm cloud instead of the
opportunities hidden in and around them.

David understood the law of if. His father sent
him to the battlefield with food for his brothers. When
he arrived he found the army hiding behind rocks.

They were afraid of Goliath, the giant that was standing in the middle of the valley.

*"A champion named Goliath, who was from Gath, came out of the Philistine camp. His height was six cubits and a span (over nine feet). He had a bronze helmet on his head and wore a coat of scale armor of bronze weighing five thousand shekels; on his legs he wore bronze greaves, and a bronze javelin was slung on his back. His spear shaft was like a weaver's rod, and its iron point weighed six hundred shekels. His shield bearer went ahead of him."* 1 Samuel 17:4-7 NIV

Wow, over nine feet tall! Goliath was much taller than the average height of a man at that time, which was five foot five inches. Imagine how big the problem must have appeared to those who looked at the giant. These men saw the crisis and the crisis decided their outcome. Their decision not to fight allowed their enemy to dictate what they could and couldn't do. They missed the door. They didn't see the potential that was standing in the middle of their life. They could not see the opportunity that was waiting to be conquered. They could have opened that door, trusted God and faced their challenge. Instead they hid like so many do. They accepted the outcome instead of using their faith. When you work your faith seasons change.

## LIFE PRINCIPLE
### *The Difference In People Is What They See.*

David had never engaged in this type of battle, but had been prepared for this day by God in the wilderness. When you spend time in God's presence, you tend to see things the way that God sees them and not the way that others see them. David had been alone in the wilderness, worshipping and singing songs to the Lord.

The Lord started a mentorship program for David's future. The Bible says a bear came out to kill David, but David rose up and killed the bear. That was Faith Building Class 101. A lion came to his camp to steal his sheep. David rose up and slew the lion; Hand to Hand Combat 102.

When David showed up on the battlefield he could hear what Goliath was saying about his God. He became angry and couldn't believe that no one would stand up and defend the name of the Lord. No one stood up because they didn't have knowledge of who the Lord really was. They were all unaware of the power of God's presence and what it felt like to be full of God's anointing. Any of them could have worked the law of "if" had they trusted God. If they would have defended God's honor they may have won the battle that day.

## LIFE PRINCIPLE
***There Is A Big Difference Between Wanting To And Willing To.***

However, it was David who recognized the opportunity. He asked what the reward was for defeating Goliath. David no longer saw the giant as a problem when he discovered the rewards. He saw an opportunity to enter his future. He operated the law of 'IF'.

David was about to change his life; he was about to live life to the fullest. The next season in his life was the palace. The same can be true for us. The difference in people is what they see. What you see decides what you say, and what you say decides what you have.

Many want to experience promotion but not everyone is willing to do what it takes to get it. That's the power of 'IF'. Think for a moment; what have you ignored that has caused your life to become stagnate instead of increasing? What have you not been willing to do? Many people wish for a lot of things, but wishing for something isn't what is required to obtain it. Wishing isn't going to give you a winner's life.

What are you willing to do right now to change? Stop wishing for a better marriage. What are you willing to do to have one? Stop wishing for a better job. What are you willing to do to obtain it? Stop wishing for a miracle. Start doing what it takes to receive one. Life is not a miracle: life is a choice. The willing always have a better life than the wishful. There's a big difference between wanting to and willing to.

## LIFE PRINCIPLE
*Increase Is Not A Bad Thing; It Is A God Thing!*

Work on your mind. Train it to control your emotions. Everyday make your mind push you toward endurance and change. Force it to become a mind that pushes your thinking to be willing to and not just wishing to.

Where do you want to go? What do you want to do? What dreams have you buried in the graveyard of yesterday? Decide right now that you are willing to do what it takes to see those dreams become a reality. Don't be afraid anymore.

Meditate on this; God wants you to increase. Phillips Brooks, a clergyman and author in the 19th century said, ***"Bad will be the day for every man when he becomes absolutely contented with the life he is leading, with the thoughts he is thinking, with the deeds he is doing; when there is not forever beating at the doors of his soul some great desire to do something larger, which he knows that he was meant and made to do, because he is still, in spite of all, the child of God."***

The desire to want more is not evil; it is a Godly desire. We must stop religious imprintings that rob us from living a winner's life. I don't believe for one minute that God intended for any human to live a life of insignificance. When wrong decisions trigger the law of unintended consequences, don't stop moving forward.

## LIFE PRINCIPLE
*Wrong Decisions Trigger The Law Of Unintended Consequences.*

I have made many decisions in my life that have cost me dearly. It would have been easy to give up on my destiny, but I continue to press towards my future.

*"I'm not saying that I have this all together, that I have it made. But I am well on my way, reaching out for Christ, who has so wondrously reached out for me. Friends, don't get me wrong: By no means do I count myself an expert in all of this, but I've got my eye on the goal, where God is beckoning us onward— to Jesus. I'm off and running, and I'm not turning back."* Philippians 3:12-14 The Message

No matter what you are facing, if you are willing to do what is necessary for change, you will reap your promise! This life principle will help you make better decisions and live a life of winning!

## CHAPTER THIRTEEN

# IT'S TIME TO RECOVER ALL

*T*here's not a person alive who hasn't experienced the deep pain and feelings of loss because of wrong choices. Proverbs 14:12 says, *"There is a way that seems right to a man, but it's end is the way of (destruction) death."* NKJV

The good news is that we serve a merciful God who wrote repentance into the equation because He knew we were flawed. God knew we would disobey, rebel and do it our own way at times.

God has more mercy in His plan than He has judgment. God wants to work with us. He desires to restore us and not to destroy us. Religion has made God out to be condemning and unforgiving. However, the Bible teaches that God loves more than He hates and forgives faster than He judges. God reaches to us as a protective father who is loving, kind and caring.

> **LIFE PRINCIPLE**
> *With God Anything Broken Can Be Repaired... Anything Closed Can Be Opened.*

God is a God of recovery. I don't care how many mistakes you have made. Confess your mess and tell God you are sorry. Accept His son, Jesus, who is our access and intercessor.

The word "recovery" is defined as *the regaining of or possibility of regaining something lost or taken away; an improvement in the economy marking the end of a recession or decline.*

## RECOVERY WITH GAIN

*Get excited! You are living in the time of recovery!* Understand that when God is involved with your recovery He makes the **enemy add interest to your loss**. You don't just recover; you recover with increase.

*"...Yet when he* (the thief or enemy) *is found, he must restore sevenfold; He may have to give up all the substance of his house."* Proverbs 6:31 NKJV

No matter what you have done, when you discover that the enemy was behind your loss, you can claim this verse for recovery through Jesus Christ. God can reverse the wrong and make it right even after a bad decision. When we repent we activate the law of mercy. Mercy is two–fold.

First, God's mercy is new every morning. *"This I recall to my mind, therefore I have hope. Through the Lord's mercies we are not consumed, Because His compassions fail not. They are new every morning; Great is your faithfulness. "The Lord is my portion," says my soul, "Therefore I hope in Him!"* Lamentations 3:21-24 NKJV

No matter what you did yesterday, when you woke up today God had brand new mercy over you. Mercy is defined as *clemency: leniency and compassion shown toward offenders by a person or agency charged with administering justice.*

Only God has the right to judge your mistakes, yet when we plead with him He's a God of mercy! God gives us clemency, leniency and above all, compassion. No one can show mercy, nor can they walk in forgiveness with anyone until they possess and move in the heart of compassion.

This is hard because we live in a cruel and cynical world; a world where everyone is competing to outperform others. Thank God He is not like that! We are to strive to be like Him, forgiving those who wounded us and living our lives in the realm of compassion...His compassion!

I must confess that I struggle at times with this one. I can be uncompassionate. My heart aches to be more like Christ. I am so weak in life. Competition is my greatest enemy. This stems from my wounds of rejection, insecurities and above all, a low self-image. Maybe you're wondering how can a person who writes books, ministers on television and pastors a church have these weak areas in his mind. I have to fight them every day. What I do doesn't help who I am. What I do is my calling. What I am has to be forged through Christ. You have to die to self to develop a healthy self-image. I have decided to build myself worth in the fact that I AM because HE WAS! Jesus is the Christ, the Anointed Redeemer, who gives me the power to be who He has destined me to be.

Every day when you open your eyes, you have entered into a new day with new decisions and with a God who wants to give you new mercy. He doesn't carry over your stupidity from yesterday.

Second, God's mercies are everlasting. *"For the Lord is good; his mercy is everlasting; and his truth endureth to all generations."* Psalm 100:5 KJV

God gives His mercy life. His mercy will live as long as He is God and He will be God forever. He has no beginning so His mercy has no beginning. God has no end so His mercy knows no end. Mercy transcends time.

## RULES FOR MERCY

God's mercy has some qualifications attached to it. *"But the mercy of the Lord is from everlasting to everlasting upon them that fear him, and his righteousness unto children's children: To such as keep his covenant, and to those that remember his commandments to do them. The Lord hath prepared his throne in the heavens; and his kingdom ruleth over all."* Psalm 103:17-19 KJV

You don't activate His mercy just because you're alive. You activate His mercy when you decide to give up who you are and obey and live by His laws. All of God's laws produce different rewards. Here are some laws for reaping the reward of mercy:

1. ***Fear Him***: Fearing God means that you know that He is awesome and worthy to be honored and obeyed. This word fear can be defined as HONOR. When we honor God we trust Him. We obey Him. We make Him our source and not man. **Honor is the key to access.** Honor gives you the reward for God's access and that access is given to you because of mercy.

2. ***Be a Covenant Keeper***: You will not receive mercy if you break God's covenant. It would be very prudent for you to learn and study all you can about the covenant and your covenant rights. You can't really pray if you don't know your covenant rights. I taught a fifteen week series on the power of covenant. You can order this teaching series on my website, www.godstrongtv.com

3. ***Remember and Obey God's Laws:*** Commands are not the same as covenant. A

covenant is a contract between two parties. Every law has a different reward, and the reward is activated in our lives through our obedience to the law. For instance, the law of confessing Jesus as Lord gives us the reward of eternal life.

Another law is the law of prosperity. Increase and wealth are the rewards for the law of prosperity. The law of prosperity is governed by principles. Obey God's principles and you will prosper.

## Laws and their Rewards:

1. Change is the reward for The Law of Adaptability.
2. Increase is the reward for the Law of Seed.
3. Growth is the reward for The Law of Change.
4. Access is the reward for The Law of Honor.
5. God's presence is the reward for The Law of Praise.
6. Miracles are the reward for The Law of Obedience.

## GOD RESTORES BECAUSE OF HIS MERCY

God wants to be recognized for His kindness and love. He wants us to know that He cares and that He is here for us. He's the father you never had, the counselor and friend that sticks closer than a brother. He's not sitting in heaven waiting for you and me to mess up. We will make mistakes and when we do, He is there with arms opened wide and a kind, warm smile on His face saying, *"Come to me, all you who are weary and burdened, and I will give you rest."* Matthew 11:28 NIV

## GOD IS A GOD OF INCREASE

God has never been about taking; He is about giving. He is about releasing. He created man in the garden and gave him dominion over the earth. This is a powerful truth. God is about restoration. He wants us to recover what we've lost.

One of my good friends recently reminded me of a verse in Psalm 78 that talks about how the people of God limited His hand of prosperity and blessings. They experienced many signs and wonders in the wilderness; bread called manna, meat that rained out of heaven, water that flowed from a rock and bitter waters turned sweet. God was with them in a cloud by day and a fire by night. They witnessed all of these miracles and yet still limited God because they were not willing to stretch their faith to receive. God was willing to release it, but they couldn't see beyond the natural.

## OUTPOURING IS ABOUT INCREASE

Increase is the proof that God has poured out His Spirit. When God enters the environment everything will grow, increase and heal. When the Holy Spirit was poured out in Acts chapter three, the church increased three thousand souls that day. Your life will experience increase every time God touches you!

## TEN KEYS TO RECOVERY

Recovery Key One: ***Take Personal Accountability***

Stop the blame game. Swiftly take the blame for your defeat. It may not be your fault, but if you keep blaming everyone else you will never move past your failure or problem. Take responsibility for your failure. Move quickly to the realization that you may have made some bad decisions and fix them yourself.

Stop rummaging through your past; all you will find is pain. Stop looking at the bad parent or the rejection that you experienced at school. Your past is over. The mistakes you are making today cannot be blamed on yesterday. You made them. You need to face them, fix them and forget them! The only thing you have control over is you. So take control!

Recovery Key Two: **Be Transparent About Your Weakness**

You don't have to broadcast your weaknesses, but make sure you don't hide them either. Most of the people around you know your failures and faults. Your weaknesses are real!

You can't use the gift of repentance if you don't confess where you've failed. Repentance is a gift. This is very powerful:

*"Come now, and let us **reason** together, saith the Lord: though your sins be as scarlet, they shall be as white as snow; though they be red like crimson, they shall be as wool. If ye be willing and obedient, ye shall eat the good of the land."* Isaiah 1:18-19 KJV

God said, *"Let us reason together..."* Let's talk about your life, your mess, your sin and your failures. The word reason means *to decide, to convict, to be convinced, to rebuke and to reprove.* God's desire is to persuade us to change by showing us where we have fallen short of His laws.

You will eat the good of the land, share in the bounty and gladness, when you come to God and allow Him to reason with you about your weaknesses.

Recovery Key Three: **Master Conversation**

Build a winner's mind! Conversation gives birth to things. Be careful that you don't talk to wrong people about your mistakes.

FACTS ABOUT WRONG PEOPLE:

1. Wrong people always give wrong advice.
2. Wrong people create wrong seasons.
3. Wrong people can cancel out God's favor.
4. Wrong people attach demonic spirits around you.

If you want something to die in your past, stop having conversation about it in your present. Your faith grows by your words. If you want to feel good and do well, learn to have good conversation.

Recovery Key Four: **Raise Your Standard**

The word standard means *guidelines, pattern and measure*. When we raise our standard we raise our guidelines. We set better parameters around us. Most failures can be traced to people doing the same thing over and over. If you want to experience something different then change your patterns.

When you raise the standard expect mediocrity to reveal itself. When you call for commitment, the uncommitted will become exposed. Expect others to leave your life, your ministry and your business when you decide to raise the standard.

Elevate your mind. If you don't elevate, you will eventually stagnate. You must get a different view of your life. To change your viewpoint, you must change your point of view.

Recovery Key Five: *Isolate Yourself From The Crowd*

Sometimes you need to be alone. Too many people in times of recovery can create confusion. There are too many opinions in a crowd. Get alone so that you can hear the voice of God. Place only a few

## LIFE PRINCIPLE
*What You Connect To You Will Eventually Become.*

people around you. The crowd always has a different agenda. Even Jesus had to get away from the multitudes. They will drain you. You can't make right decisions hanging around the crowd. Get alone so that you will hear clearly.

Recovery Key Six: *Monitor Your Connections And Friends*

When God wants to bless you, He'll schedule the right people to connect too. When Satan wants to destroy you, he'll find the wrong person to connect you to.

When God implements protection He'll remove wrong people in your life. When you see people leaving your life don't panic! When something or someone is leaving your life the law of displacement is at work. That law is that if something is trying to enter your life it's forcing what's already in your life to leave. Be cautious that you don't become so focused on the people exiting your life that you miss the greater relationships that are attempting to enter.

When you are in agreement with a rebel, you will reap a rebel's reward. I can reap through agreement the rebels reward... then the truth has to work in the positive as well as the negative. Connection, agreement unlocks the law of flow. What is flowing in those around you will eventually flow to you and through you. *A great rule for life is to qualify before you trust.* The power in connection, the power in agreement... One can send a thousand... but two in agreement increase the power of potential to ten thousand. You may be reaping a consequence that has nothing to do with your life style. But has everything to do with your friendships or connections.

The most important connection you can make is with someone who will build your faith, ignite your passion and protect your focus. A person who is willing to see your flaws and mentor you past them is your greatest asset.

Recovery Key Seven: *Never Resist Transition And Change*

Change is uncomfortable and isn't easy. Change without transition is merely rearrangement. Deciding to change without the willingness to make transition is like rearranging your furniture. Moving the couch doesn't make your house new.

*Change is situational...transition is psychological.*

The word transition means to be transformed. We see this word in Romans chapter 12 *"... and do not be conformed to this world, **but be transformed by the renewing of your mind**, that you may prove what is that good and acceptable and perfect will of God."* Romans 12:2 NKJV

The word transformed is translated from the word metamorphose. Think about the caterpillar which becomes imprisoned in the cocoon. What seems like prison is only the shell of change and transition. While inside the cocoon the caterpillar is becoming what it was always destined to be. A caterpillar's view is limited to the ground. They crawl on their bellies and eat the dust of the earth. Their movement is slow and sluggish, but that is just its beginning stage. Its destiny is much greater. The caterpillar builds its cocoon and imprisons itself inside for a season of change. If it can survive this season it will metamorphosize into something completely different.

The word metamorphoses means *to change in appearance, structure, character and reactions.*

We don't really change until we transform, and we can't transform until we renew our minds. You must train your mind to think better thoughts. Your mind is a gift from God. It has the power to magnify whatever you focus on. This is how ordinary people can do extraordinary things. Train your mind to focus on the right things. If you don't, it will continue to make the bad things bigger and the good things in your future smaller.

When we transform and metamorphosize, we stop crawling and eating the dust of others. We are no longer sluggish and slow. The caterpillar becomes the butterfly. We have broken free from the cocoon and now we can fly. The level of our focus has changed and our life has been accelerated to greater heights!

**There are three stages to change:**

STAGE ONE: *The Letting Go Stage*

You must let go of some major areas.
1. Old identities
2. Old relationships
3. Old habits
4. Old mindsets

The letting go stage will produce a feeling of loss in us that will stop this process immediately if not dealt with. Anyone who is attempting to make change must be prepared to experience a momentary sense of loss. Don't be moved by this feeling. Your willingness to let go of the wrong influences will make room for the right things to enter your life.

STAGE TWO: *Transition Stage*

This stage is the hardest to me because it is a wilderness season. It is a place you have never experienced before. The old has gone but the new has not yet arrived. If you don't keep moving in one direction then you will begin to doubt your change and do what the children of Israel did. You will start to question God and get stuck in the wilderness.

## LIFE PRINCIPLE
*The Wilderness Is The Opportunity For New Beginnings.*

The wilderness is a place of death. The old habits, the old ways and the old mind sets have to die. The wilderness is the graveyard where these things are buried. You kill them so they don't torment you in the Promised Land.

Don't try to keep alive what God is trying to kill. If you try to keep the past alive, you will prolong your winter and cause your wilderness living to last longer than God had planned. Even though this can be the most dangerous place for change, it can also be the best place for opportunity. Your mind begins to shift and starts to build a different pattern of thinking.

Winter may look like death and have the appearance of sadness. However, winter is the time where your roots are being replenished and strengthened. It is in winter where healing takes place at the inner level. Everything on the surface looks dead, but it is alive. The root system is growing, repairing and waiting on spring's arrival.

It is during this dark season that we disengage from yesterday's failures, memories and pain and are preparing to connect to tomorrow's greatness and change.

**Facts To Remember While Going Through Transition:**

1. *Be very cautious of those who approach you in this season.* You are vulnerable to wrong voices.
2. *Be very selective in your relationships.* People will decide which part of you grows and which part of you dies. Voices decide your faith or your doubts. Friends will feed either your weaknesses or your strengths.

3. ***Don't live for popularity in this season; learn to be alone for a time.*** Popularity is when others like you, but happiness is when you like you.

4. ***When the Divine Presence is hindered so is divine reward.*** Don't allow your attitude to weaken. Stay in your secret place. Keep an attitude of thankfulness and praise. You want to keep God's presence around you, no matter what.

5. ***Practice the Word of God. Use the Word of God often.*** God's word will demoralize demonic attack over your mind. Use faith talk and not doubt talk.

6. ***Master your conversation.*** Stop discussing what you want to die in your past. Your conversations may be keeping it alive in your present and affecting your future. Remember, every conversation gives birth to something good or something bad.

7. ***Decide that you will survive this season, no matter what.*** Make up your mind that, no matter what, you will be willing to do what it takes to change. Sometimes you must learn how to survive. Don't try to make advancements...just make sure you survive. If you survive you will thrive again.

8. ***Willingness is a powerful law.*** There is a big difference between wanting to and willing to. Many want to quit a habit. Many want to change. Many want to have a better home and better finances, but few are willing to do what it takes to have it. I heard a story about a person whose business began to suffer. This person decided to take a job that was beneath their skill level so that the bills would be paid. They

worked the law of willing to. Their company started to grow again and never had to work the other job!

STAGE THREE: **YOU'VE CHANGED! YOU'RE GOING INTO THE PROMISED LAND!**

Remember, there may be giants in your next season. Giants are the proof that you've entered the Promised Land.

Recovery Key Eight: **Develop And Customize A Life Of Obedience.**

When God is ready to increase and bless you, He will give you an instruction. Many times those instructions will come through a man or woman of God. Change and increase are the result of an obeyed instruction. If you can't weather the season of correction and instruction then you will be stuck in your present season forever!

Recovery Key Nine: **Develop The Law Of Persistency**

Persistency means you keep trying. You must value your assignment and your commitment to recover, more than you value the opinions of others if you are going to be persistent. Don't think that everyone around you is excited about your decision to recover. Most of those around you will try to talk you out of your decision. You must decide right now to be persistent. Endurance is a qualifier.

Recovery Key Ten: **Swiftly Change Your Seed**

If you don't like your present harvest, then change your seed. Your seed decides what harvest you are in position to receive. If you want a financial harvest in your next season then sow seeds of money in this season. If you want your marriage to have a better harvest in its next season, then sow the seeds of time and interest in this season. Sow the seed to obtain whatever harvest you want to reap.

The whole earth is pregnant with harvest. Seeds are the only voices that the earth will respond to. God made it that way. *"Be not deceived; God is not mocked: for whatsoever a man soweth, that shall he also reap"* (Galatians 6:7 KJV). So many people refuse to activate the law of seed time and harvest, even though the proof of it can be seen all around them in nature.

Each one of God's laws has a different reward attached to them. There are some things that God will not release until you've decided to get involved with your life and change. God has been waiting on you. He wants you to recover all!

## CHAPTER FOURTEEN

# HOW TO GET YOUR EDGE BACK

## THE STRENGTH TO BRING FORTH!

*"...This day is a day of trouble, and rebuke, and blasphemy; for the children have come to birth, but there is no strength to bring them forth."* 2 Kings 19:3-4 NKJV

When I read this verse I began to see a clear picture of why so many in our churches have sad faces and blank stares. They have been carrying their promise, their baby, for years. They leave their Sunday worship service week after week full of word... full of promise... full of wanting more and doing more, but never coming to full term. Notice in the verse that trouble, rebuke and blasphemy are the results of not giving birth.

Frustration can enter your life when you are unable to birth your promise. Many people have learned to accept their life instead of change it. This is why religion doesn't work. Religion causes you to go through the "motions of church" but never produce in you that which God has called you to!

Many in the church have become weary, angry and tired from carrying their promise for so many years. Imagine a woman being pregnant for as many years as some people have been carrying their promise. Nine months seems like forever to a pregnant lady! Some have been in church for years and still have not yet found the strength to bring forth.

We've become a bitter, broke and non - productive people in this last day ,twenty-first century church; going through the motions of life week after week but without joy, excitement, expectation or the willingness to believe for more. Many are full of trouble, rebuke and blasphemy. I hear phrases like,

*"Why bother?" "Why give?" "Why lift my hands and praise?" "Things aren't going to change."* The eyes of these people are hollow, and their stare is a cold, non-responsive look; as if they've become hypnotized to a set of actions and emotionless ways.

**I declare not so!** The world says we are to accept who we are and that's it; play the hand that you've been dealt. The church says that if you don't like that hand then you're ungrateful and not content. But I don't believe that's true. We can be who God's called us to be. We can have more, do more and be more. I am done with shouting about the future but never possessing it. I am ready to wake up from Adam's nightmares and start living in God's dreams.

## LIFE PRINCIPLE
*You Have Become Larger Than Your Present Season.*

**How about you?**

**The effects of carrying your promise too long:**

*"But as one was cutting down a tree, the iron ax head fell into the water; and he cried out and said, "Alas, master! For it was borrowed." So the man of God said, "Where did it fall?" And he showed him the place. So he cut off a stick, and threw it in there; and he made the iron float. Therefore he said, "Pick it up for yourself." So he reached out his hand and took it."*
2 Kings 6:5-7 NKJV

You will go through the motions but **lose your edge** when you carry your promise too long.

Your frustrations are not evil. As a matter of fact, I believe they are God directed. If you are feeling

(139)

that the place in which you now live is too small then you have become larger than your present season. Now you are ready to give birth.

The story in 2 Kings chapter six tells us that the sons of the prophets came to the man of God and said, **"The place in which we dwell is too small. Let us move."** Let us build a bigger place. This is a sign that the season of birthing is on you. This readiness to become bigger is God sent. You are experiencing the pressure of living in a small season when you've been destined for bigger and better things.

But what happened? While one was working to get into his future, the axe head fell off of the axe handle. He was now working but had no edge. The axe head is the key to movement; the key to production and success. The axe head is the proof that we have the edge in our efforts to win. This man was working but had LOST HIS EDGE.

## HAVE YOU LOST YOUR EDGE?

Abraham Lincoln was once asked a question about what would be his plan of action if he were given eight hours to chop down a tree. He replied, *"I would spend seven hours sharpening my axe."* Wow! Think on that; he was willing to spend seven hours of preparation for one hour of work. The church is just the opposite. We will spend seven hours trying to produce with one hour of preparation. **The only place mediocrity shines is in the church.**

Many people have lost their edge. They keep going to church, going to work, living their lives but never stopping to look for what has been lost in the process. Their love for life is lost. Their edge is gone.

The ax handle is swinging but there is no production in the process.

People who have lost their edge are at best bruising the tree in front of them, hurting those around them and hating those who are trying to help

---

**LIFE PRINCIPLE**
*It Seems That The Only Place Mediocrity Shines Is In The Church.*

---

them.

This man stopped and cried out, *"Master, I've lost my edge. My axe head has slipped off. While I was working, something happened."* This is life and sometimes life just causes you to lose your edge.

Look at how things transpire. The Man of God asked him a question. **"Where did you lose it?"** Show me! That one revelation is powerful to me. Until you can show God where you lost your edge, God can't and won't put it back.

The man replied, *"Master, it fell into the Jordan."* The prophet cut down a branch and threw it in the Jordan. That branch is a type of Christ.

*"There shall come forth a Rod from the stem of Jesse, and a Branch shall grow out of his roots. The Spirit of the Lord shall rest upon Him, The Spirit of wisdom and understanding, The Spirit of counsel and might, The Spirit of knowledge and of the fear of the Lord."*
Isaiah 11:1-2 NKJV

REVERSE PHYSICS: The iron head floated....

When you are willing and able to point out the place where you lost your edge, you will position yourself for a miracle. You are ready for restoration.

The supernatural will fall into your atmosphere. God will now do what is uncommon. In the natural, iron doesn't float, but God changed the laws of physics. God made the water give back the axe head. When the iron began to float, the prophet told the man to go down into the water and get it for himself.

No one can get your edge back for you. You are going to have to get down into the mud and mess for a moment to retrieve it for yourself. Let me give you some keys to getting your edge back so that you can live the winner's life.

## KEY ONE: YOU MUST SURVIVE THE SEASON OF STRUGGLE AND TROUBLE.

You must understand that the proof you are ready to enter your next season will usually be struggle. Trouble is the sign you have now become bigger than your present season. Storms are not sent by God to destroy you. God hides His rain in storm clouds. If you are not careful, you will try to rebuke the storm; you will command it to cease. However, God has hidden His presence, His rain and His promotion in the storm that you have been rebuking. This could be the reason you haven't received your outpouring.

## KEY TWO: YOU MUST PUSH PAST FAILURE.

How does a body builder get bigger? He works his muscles to failure so that they get bigger and stronger. How does a runner train for a marathon? He will run to the point of failure and train his mind and body to ignore the pain so that he can run further.

There's a story in Luke chapter six where Jesus talked about the enemy. He said if your enemy hits you on the right cheek then give him your left cheek. If he takes your coat then give him your shirt. If he makes you walk a mile then you walk two miles.

I once wondered if God was asking us to be cowards; to bow down and allow the enemy free reign over us. I have learned that this is not so. Jesus was trying to tell us there is more in us than that! When the enemy punches you in the face then turn your cheek, look him in the eye and ask, *"Is that all you got? Here, hit me again."*

## LIFE PRINCIPLE
*You Are A Two-Mile Person Living In A One-Mile World.*

When the enemy asks for your coat, let him know he can have your shirt, too. When he pushes you to the mile marker, and everyone around you is exhausted and quitting, keep stepping forward. You have more in you. You are a two-mile person living in a one-mile world.

FACTS ABOUT FAILURE:
1. Failure is necessary.
2. Failure creates the desire for success.
3. Without failure success would have no meaning.
4. Everyone who has succeeded has had to push past failure.

### KEY THREE: WORK THE MASTER MIND PRINCIPLE.

No one on the earth was made to succeed alone. God said it wasn't good for man to be alone so He created Eve to be with Adam in the garden. That was when the law of two started. I call it the law of agreement.

*"...that if two of you agree on earth concerning anything that they ask, it will be done for them by My Father in heaven. For where two or three are gathered together in My name, I am there in the midst of them."* Matthew 18:19-20 NKJV

One of us can chase a thousand but two of us in agreement will increase to ten thousand times stronger (Deuteronomy 32:30). Find those who are in agreement to your future and not speaking against it. You will not succeed alone. Find those who want to agree with your dreams. Build alliances to your dreams. This is called the science of success. I call it the law of divine connection.

If one can produce a thousand and by just adding someone else it can increase your potential to ten thousand, think about what happens if you attach to someone who disagrees with your dreams and visions. You may decrease ten thousand.

## KEY FOUR: KNOW YOUR DEFINITE PURPOSE.

Chapter one dealt with this. Until you know your difference you will never know your purpose. The prosperity of God is assigned to your purpose.

## KEY FIVE: TAKE POSSESSION OF YOUR OWN MIND.

Your mind is your world. I probably write and say this phrase more than any other. I am very passionate about this law. Your mind has to be dealt with or you will not win. To get your life back, take possession of your own thoughts.

Dale Carnegie believed this. He once said that he believed every human was handed two envelopes at birth. One envelope read, "The reward you will receive if you possess the power of your own mind"; the other read, "The penalty if you don't."

THE REWARDS FOR TAKING POSSESSION OF YOUR OWN MIND:
1. Good health
2. Sound and peaceful mind
3. A labor of love of your choice
4. Freedom from fear and worry
5. A positive mental attitude throughout life
6. Material riches of your own choosing and quantity

Wow! I love that list.

THE PENALTY IF YOU DON'T TAKE POSSESSION OF YOUR OWN MIND:
1. Ill health
2. Fear and worry
3. Indecisions and doubt
4. Frustration and discouragement throughout life
5. Poverty and want
6. A whole list of evils; envy, lust, greed, jealousy, hatred, un-forgiveness, bitterness, and superstitions.

***KEY SIX: KNOWING GOD'S PLAN IS NOT ENOUGH. YOU MUST EXECUTE GOD'S PLAN.***

Many know the plan... many have sat down and studied the plan... but few have decided to work and live out the plan. Faith without works is dead. When you execute the plan, the plan will execute the enemy.

God doesn't anoint a man (person). He anoints the plan then finds the man who is willing to work the plan. When that person begins to execute God's plan, the plan of God allows him or her to be anointed to accomplish the plan.

Jeremiah 29:11 tells us that God knows the plans He as for us. We must learn, discern and then embrace the plan. I believe that prosperity is not following us, but waiting on us. Money is waiting on us to discover the plan. When we make the decision to get involved in the plan, God will reveal money to us. Let me be clear - the money is to accomplish the plans of God!

### KEY SEVEN: YOU CAN'T CHANGE YOUR LIFE UNTIL YOU CHANGE YOUR PERSUASION.

## LIFE PRINCIPLE
**Faith Doesn't Just Believe That God Can; It Believes That God will.**

I have discovered two things about people:

1. You can only **move** in life at the level of your persuasion.
2. You can only **receive** in life at the level of your persuasion.

Persuasion is defined as *a deep conviction, an inner belief system, a knowing*. When you are persuaded, you have this inner conviction and belief that God is going to bring you out to bring you in! It is your faith! Faith doesn't just believe that God can. It's easy to say God can. Of course He can; He's God. So to say that you believe God can heal, deliver and bring you financial increase isn't really saying that you have faith. The enemy knows that God can. This speaks to the ability of God, but doesn't speak to the willingness of God. The persuaded believe that God is and that God will.

*"But without faith it is impossible to please Him, for he who comes to God must believe that He is, and that He is a rewarder of those who diligently seek Him."* Hebrews 11:6 NKJV

7 PERSUASIONS YOU NEED TO POSSESS:

1. **In everything, victory is going to be the end result.**
2. **The only part of God's Word that works for you will be the part you believe.**
3. **Prosperity is Godly.**
4. **It's not wrong to expect to receive from God after you have sown your seeds to God.**
5. **Your faith can produce anything you believe it can.**
6. **Salvation wasn't the only thing Jesus accomplished on the cross.** There were three things placed on the cross. Sin, sickness and poverty. The solution to sin is confession. We receive salvation when we confess that Jesus is the Son of God, He died for our sins and arose from the dead (Romans 10:9). The answer to sickness is our faith. The prayer of faith will bring healing when we believe in the

healing power of His blood. By Jesus' stripes we are healed (Isaiah 53). The answer to poverty is prosperity.

## 7. God rewards those who are persuaded that He will!

Faith and reasoning cannot exist in the same mind. Benjamin Franklin said you can't have faith and reasoning in the same room. Either we are going to work this out through human reasoning or we are going to have faith to believe. If we are going to work our faith then we must throw out the mental power of reasoning.

Which is it? Are you going to believe or are you going to keep trying to figure it out?

You are not required to know how God is going to bring your edge back or how He is going to bring forth your promise. You are only required to believe that He can and He will!

## Conclusion

My prayer and desire is that all of God's people will live life to its fullest. Stop accepting your life the way it is and start believing for better.

We are full of potential, but potential means nothing if it is not tapped.

My son came home from football practice one afternoon. He was beaming from ear to ear. He looked at me and said, *"Dad, the coach told me today that I am full of potential."*

I looked at him and replied, *"Son, you know what the coach was really telling you?"*

*"No,"* he said.

*"You are doing nothing. You have the ability to be and do better. You can have more and play more if you would only tap into what's inside of you."*

I hope that you will stop living in potential and begin to tap into the greatness that is inside of you. You only have one life to live...***Live It To Win It!***

Dr. G

## ABOUT THE AUTHOR

Dr. Grillo is a life coach and well-known conference and motivational speaker. He has been uniquely gifted and anointed by God to bring healing and restoration to hurting individuals, fragmented families and discouraged leaders to the nation and around the world.

Dr. Grillo spent fourteen years in youth ministry after completing his studies from Southeastern University in Lakeland, Florida. Through circumstances early in his ministry experience, God placed in Dr. Grillo a deep burning to reach into the pit of life and pull out those that religion had discarded as unreachable and valueless.

Dr. Jerry Grillo founded **The Favor Center** in 1994, a place of healing and restoration for those looking for a God who is more than just a Savior, but Lord, in every aspect of life. This has remained the focal point of his passion in ministry and the driving force of The Favor Center Churches.

Dr. Grillo holds a Bachelor of Arts in Pastoral Ministry and a Masters in Pastoral Ministry from Christian Bible College and Seminary in Independence, Missouri. Dr. Grillo holds a Doctorate of Divinity from St. Thomas Christian College. He also is a member of the AACC (American Association of Christian Counseling).

Dr. Grillo and his wife, Maryann, have been married since 1988. Together, they have a son, Jerry, III and daughter, Jordan.

## *May I Invite You To Make Jesus Christ The Lord Of Your Life?*

The Bible says, *"That if you will confess with your mouth the Lord Jesus, and will believe in your heart that God raised Him from the dead, you will be saved. For with the heart man believes unto righteousness; and with the mouth confession is made for salvation."* Romans 10:9 &10

**Pray this prayer with me today:**

*"Dear Jesus, I believe that You died for me and rose again on the third day. I confess to You that I am a sinner. I need Your love and forgiveness. Come into my life, forgive my sins and give me eternal life. I confess You now as my Lord. Thank You for my salvation! I walk in Your peace and joy from this day forward. Amen!"*

Signed_____

Date

_____

### [*Mail this in to Dr. Grillo*]

☐ Yes Dr. Jerry, I made a decision to accept Christ as my personal Savior today, and I would like to be placed on your mailing list.

Name_____

Address_____

City_____ State _____ Zip _____

Phone_____Email_____

### FOGZONE MINISTRIES
P.O. Box 3707, Hickory N.C. 28603
Toll Free 888.328.6763 * Email prayer@godstrongtv.com

Dear Friend,

I know God has brought us together…Your partnership will be very valuable to spread the Gospel around the world.

Our ministry is growing and presently reaching over 100 million people every week. According to Mark 10:29, when we get involved with God's business – giving up time, money, and possessions for the Gospel's sake – Jesus said He would give it back 100-Fold!

*Partnership is one of God's greatest laws for financial and spiritual exchange…*what you connect to you will eventually become.

I assure you that I am anointed for favor and to heal the broken, and when God is blessing me, you can expect your partnership to create your next season for favor and healing.

I ask God every day to send those who he has assigned to partner with my ministry. Would you ask the Holy Spirit if you are one of those God has chosen to partner with me in healing the broken, encouraging the weak and saving the lost?

If you are, read over the partnership plan and stretch your faith…faith always changes seasons! I have asked God to give you a harvest of FAVOR, FINANCIAL INCREASE, and FAMILY RESTORATION!

Thank you in advance for partnering with me…you will definitely see the reward!

Dr. Jerry Grillo

## PARTNERSHIP PLAN

**300 Favored Champion Partner:** _____ Yes, Dr. Grillo I want to be one of your Favored Champion Partners of **$24.00 a month**; Gideon had 300 who helped him conquer the enemy. I want to be one of the 300 who partner with you to conquer the enemy of lack.

**70 Favored Elders:** _____ Yes, Dr. Grillo I want to be one of your 70 Favored Elders of **$84.00 a month**. I want to be one of those who will help lift your arms so that we can win over the enemy of fear and failure.

**My Best Monthly Seed: $_____.____** Remember, no seed is too small and all seeds multiply. Seeds of nothing will produce harvests of nothing. Send you best seed today.

Name_____

Address_____

City _____State_____zip_____

Phone _____Email

_____

*Write Your Most Pressing NEED Below!*

_____

_____

_____

_____

_____

### *WHAT YOU CAN EXPECT BY BEING A MONTHLY FAVORED PARTNER.*

When you become a Favored Monthly Partner, you can expect to receive my Favored Partner Pack:

1. **A MONTHLY NEWSLETTER AND WEEKLY EBLASTS WITH MINISTRY UPDATES.**

2. **MONTHLY DVD'S FROM SERVICES AT THE FAVOR CENTER.**

3. **DR. GRILLO AND HIS INTERCESSORY TEAM WILL BE PRAYING WITH YOU OVER YOUR NEEDS.**

4. **PERSONALLY SIGNED COPIES OF DR. GRILLO'S NEWEST RELEASED BOOKS FREE OF CHARGE.**

5. **VIP SEATING AT ANY "FAVOR CONNECTION CONFERENCE".**

6. **VIP SEATING AT DR. GRILLO'S CHURCH – THE FAVOR CENTER.**

7. **25 % DISCOUNT ON ALL FOGZONE PRODUCTS.**

Don't hesitate...I am excited to hear from you. Thank you for your support. The seed that leaves your hand, doesn't leave your life...it enters your future where it multiplies into your harvest.

I speak the Favor of God over you and know that your partnership is already creating your harvest. You are going to be a part of the end time harvest of souls.

Made in the USA
Monee, IL
11 February 2022

90344659R00085